23RD PRECINCT
THE JOB

23RD PRECINCT
THE JOB

ARLENE SCHULMAN

The names of some police officers
and civilians have been changed.

Copyright © 2001 by Arlene Schulman

Published by
Soho Press, Inc.
853 Broadway
New York, N.Y. 10003

Library of Congress Cataloging-in-Publication Data
Schulman, Arlene
    23rd precinct : the job / Arlene Schulman.
        p. cm
    ISBN 1-56947-237-8 (alk. paper)
    1. Police—New York (N.Y.) 2. Crime—New York (N.Y.)

HV8148.N5 S385 2001
363.2'09747'1—dc21   00-067968

Manufactured in the United States
10 9 8 7 6 5 4 3 2 1

To the men and women of the 23rd Precinct

Contents

Along for the Ride

Who are these people who wear uniforms, carry guns and patrol our streets? What is it like to be a cop? Who wants to be one and why? I wanted to know.

Would the New York City Police Department allow itself to be examined on a daily basis? I wrote a letter to John Miller, Deputy Commissioner of Public Information of the Police Department under Police Commissioner William Bratton. I requested permission to spend a year in a Manhattan precinct, riding with police officers on patrol—a neighborhood's first link to law and order. Miller recognized that access to the Department might result in good public relations and more balanced media coverage. He said yes.

I was even allowed to pick the precinct. There were seventy-six to choose from. I selected the 23rd, just north of the wealthy and powerful Upper East Side of Manhattan and just before Harlem. Two hundred police officers, working in three shifts, were responsible for it. The neighborhood stretches from Fifth Avenue to the East River, 96th Street to 115th Street, and it has everything: million-dollar apartments, drug dens, a cash-strapped city hospital and one of the best in the country, housing projects, brownstones, methadone programs, community centers, day care centers, and an ever-changing population of immigrants—Dominican, Mexican, African, South American, and Asian. It contains people who'd like to move out of the projects, others waiting to get in, and a population with one of the highest AIDS and asthma rates in the country. It's one of the most impoverished neighborhoods in New York City.

One of John Miller's lieutenants recommended that I introduce myself to the commanding officer of the 23rd Precinct, Captain Robert Curley, a large man with dark hair and glasses who loved chatting about boxing, jazz, and his two teenagers. He suggested that if I wanted to learn what a police department is really like, I read Joseph Heller's *Catch-22*, about the absurdities and bureaucracy faced by men in battle.

While Captain Curley was advised of my project, he received no specific guidelines from the Deputy Commissioner's office, only an order that I would be part of his precinct for the next twelve months. I chose who to ride with, who to interview, who to walk with. Nothing appeared to be off-limits except for Captain Curley's request that I not ride with two cops who had been under departmental investigation for firing their guns—one at a clock, the other at her boyfriend. (Unfortunately, both had hit their targets.)

I went out with all three shifts—from the midnight to 7 a.m. tour; the day tour from 7 a.m. to 3:30 p.m.; and from 3:30 p.m.

to midnight. I responded with police officers to calls about domestic violence; drug dealing and overdoses; homicides; disputes involving fists, knives, and guns; missing persons; stolen cars, wallets, and bikes; burglaries; emotionally disturbed people threatening suicide; apartment lockouts; loud radios; and people brandishing shotguns, handguns, rifles, and bayonets. I also got to know their police counterparts who specialized in guns, robberies, assaults, and homicides—the detectives.

In New York, outsiders—civilians—almost never ride with cops for an extended length of time. At best, they may scan police radios and show up at crime scenes, looking for photos and quotes. They are often thwarted. The Giuliani administration, for instance, would not have granted such access, I am convinced.

A year passed, however, and I continued my work. No one told me not to. Captain Curley had moved to another command, his tenure completed. Three more captains came and went but I remained, from 1995 through the beginning of 1997, riding with, interviewing and observing all units of the 23rd Precinct, until at last someone concluded that I shouldn't be there.

I wore a bulletproof vest and rode in the backseat of patrol cars, trying to blend in as much as possible. I saw the aggravation, the fear, and the frustration that police officers deal with every day.

To most cops, East Harlem was a foreign city—not because of where people lived but how they lived. The disputes over drugs and stolen welfare checks, the pettiness and the frustration of people made the cops—and me—wonder where the reality was. Many of the people we saw were drunk, drugged, mentally disturbed, angry, and defeated. Those genuinely looking for help often got mixed in with the rest. There weren't many with business suits on. Yet, it seemed the poorest man had a Tommy Hilfiger outfit, a car, and a complaint. Women beat each other up, their daughters did the same. People shot and killed each other for reasons they thought made perfect sense. People lied and didn't understand why they had been arrested, even when they had a gun in their hands. "It's not mine," they would protest.

It was tiring, confusing, frustrating, aggravating, unnecessary. Both the arrested and the arrestee felt the same way toward each other. I identified with both sides and it often seemed surreal to be in a world where a natural death was a drug overdose. It was as if you had to peel off a heavy layer of deceitful, dangerous grime to find any of the good parts and the good people of the neighborhood.

I, too, became afraid of being accidentally shot by nervous rookies and bored when the radio and the night were quiet. I listened to gripes about the politics of the precinct, and had no choice once when two cops I rode with insisted that a suspect threw a gun out of his car window during a chase—"You saw the same thing that we did, didn't you?" I would have been mistrusted had I not. I questioned a free soda from a poor bodega owner when a cop said, "Don't worry, take it," and wondered why I received a discount when someone else had to make a living.

I learned to look up after exiting a patrol car, uncertain if bottles, bricks, or garbage would be thrown at us from rooftops. I heard the sound of gunshots, saw the look of hatred on the faces of teenagers who think they're immortal, heard the curses of drug dealers fighting with cops when they're arrested. Everyday occurrences. I learned to use the radio, and where the nearest emergency room was. Sometimes the partners and I worked out contingencies for violent scenarios.

After two or three weeks, many forgot that I was there. It bespoke great confidence and honesty from people working in such a stressful profession. I viewed their flaws and their courage, fear and heroism, patience and impatience, honor and dishonor. I noticed people working on their own time and others not working when they should have been. I rode with rookies, nervous and raw, unprepared and untested in dealing with the battleground both on the streets and in the Police Department; women battling to be taken seriously; weary veterans counting down the years, months, and days until they retired; men who loved each other like brothers; men and women who feared or hated each other.

The Police Department is not an easy place to work, and sometimes the pressure is greater inside than outside. One thing I learned is that there's no such thing as an absolute truth. Situations change daily and people changed, and continue to change with them as a result of their experiences.

Most of all, I found that the "blue wall" is penetrable. It's not a mask of molded, expressionless faces, of men and women of all the same height, size, temperament, and personality. Each man and woman had their own particular work habits, reactions to people and events, family lives, sensitivities, and sensibilities. "The Police Department is one large dysfunctional family" was a phrase that I heard often. But even dysfunctional families manage, and they did.

Tour

"Being a cop is a culture, it's a way of life. You did
nothing before. You have no time for a fuckin' schedule. Your life
is this job. You become the culture," insists Sergeant Charlie Columbo. "I can walk down the street in any neighborhood and people
say, 'Here comes a fuckin' pig.' A lot of young kids don't have
what it takes to become a cop. I'm a cop. You live it, breathe it,
you fuckin' bleed it. Intelligence is a rarity on this job. You need
adrenaline and excitement. Once in a blue moon, you'll get it.

"There isn't a guy on this job with fuckin' time who doesn't
need a psychiatrist. The Job doesn't want to recognize what happens to us." Sergeant Columbo pauses to light a cigarette. "Most

cops are crazy. If you weren't when you come on, you become crazy. The first person through that door is me. No one's getting hurt except for me. It's my responsibility. It's a combination of responsibility and worthlessness.

"I'm not going to let someone with three years [on the job] get killed, or someone with four kids. I know that if I go through the door first, that everyone behind me will be okay. On the job I've had a concussion and broke my leg twice. They can't fuckin' kill me. I'll die from smoking."

The 23rd Precinct stationhouse was built on 102nd Street between Lexington Avenue and Third Avenue, in Manhattan, in the 1970s as a combination police station and firehouse. No matter how many times the cleaner sweeps, disinfects, and polishes, the place never looks clean. And when a group of junkies is brought in by Narcotics, the air becomes foul with body odor that permeates the first floor and foyer.

"Hey, we got a ripe one in here!" shouts the desk sergeant, who lights a cigar to counter the odor. Although smoking is technically forbidden inside a city building, no one complains, even cops with asthma.

A neatly dressed fiftyish Hispanic man in a gray suit, with too-long cuffs and a matching fedora, is standing at the complaint window, complaining that neighborhood kids stuck their tongues out at him. "Why don't you stick your tongue out at them?" suggests Officer Miranda Mays, raising her eyebrows. The man thinks it over and exits without a word. A huddle of girls slams through the front doors. A dozen, the oldest about eleven, push and shove each other in a spinning circle, one girl's mother in the middle, all punching and shouting and landing in front of Officer Bobby Pacino.

"Whoa!" exclaims the startled cop.

"Out! Out!" shouts a sergeant, and in one spinning move, they leave as quickly as they had arrived.

Pacino is seated at the so-called telephone switchboard, which is actually a pair of push-button phones with red, blinking hold buttons. Calls will come from district attorneys, cops, police officials, family, friends, neighborhood residents, and cranks. He sits behind the desk made of worn oak. It stretches almost across the length of the room, standing five feet off the floor, with a metal railing running along it. Governed by a desk sergeant or lieutenant who would be responsible for arrests, paperwork, and coordinating cops, the desk is perpetually covered with papers, in and out boxes, two grimy closed-circuit monitors, police radios that look like walkie talkies, and coffee containers. An American flag, folded into a triangle and framed under glass, and photographs of the latest police commissioner and his chiefs, hang behind the desk. Dingy green metal file cabinets line the wall. The sweet smell of angel dust from a drug safe mingles with the body odor and cigar smoke.

Bobby Pacino stands at the telephone switchboard, holding the telephone receiver to his ear. "Ma'am! Ma'am!" he says into the phone. "I don't know what to tell you. . . . Ma'am! I can't help you. This is the New York City Police Department. If the voices are coming through your TV set, call the TV repair company. Have a good evening!"

"Oh, my hair!" sighs a cop, adjusting his thinning hair. "Or lack thereof." He waits for the desk sergeant to sign in his arrest. "I got this guy for disorderly conduct, for resisting arrest. And existing arrest," he informs the sergeant. "For being an asshole."

Just across from the desk, Sergeant Kevin O'Rourke handles roll call, reminding the ranks of veterans and rookies about how to fill out arrest and stop-and-frisk reports, complaining of incomplete information, poor grammar and spelling on previous submissions. Called 61s, arrest reports detail the names and addresses of criminals and victims, and outline time, place, and occurrence.

"There has to be a story. Put it in chronological order. Fill the story out. Actions of victim—fill that out," he instructs, sounding impatient. "What were they doing? Standing on the street corner? Mark that down. Let's make the sixty-ones more complete. Maybe I can offer you a little help. Stop us. Let us see the sixty-ones. If you get hit with an object, that's an Assault Two. Everyone has a vest?"

His squad taps their chests in affirmation. Anything on this four-to-twelve watch will be his responsibility.

He mentions cops committing suicide. "In case you haven't heard, and if you want to talk about anything, that shit stays with me. You have someone to talk to."

With his dark Irish looks and thick brush of a mustache, Sergeant O'Rourke looks as if he stepped out of Teddy Roosevelt's days as police commissioner a century earlier. A former cop in the Emergency Services Unit before he was promoted, O'Rourke is accustomed to dealing with far more serious crises, like suicidal jumpers, people trapped in cars and apartments, and building collapses.

"It's like a juggling act," O'Rourke says of his new role. "You have to deal with every cop as an individual. Some think that they're in high school or on some sort of sightseeing trip. I've had people say that if it weren't for the money, they wouldn't be here. And there are police families: you do what your father did."

O'Rourke became a cop like his father, a retired detective.

"I always loved this job," he says enthusiastically. "When Dad joined in 1964, it was still a romantic job. The kids in the neighborhood in Queens knew that your father's a cop. It was almost like a status symbol."

While he completes roll call and his squad lines up for radios and car keys, a sad-eyed pooch observes the scene from the back of the room, a stray from the streets. An officer grabs a can of Alpo from the kitchen and feeds it to the dog on a paper plate.

"Well, that's one redeeming quality that you have," someone quips wryly. "You like animals."

Walter McKenney, a cop for over twenty years, stands behind the desk. He is to be Sergeant O'Rourke's designated driver.

"He's had two thousand years on the Job," says a patrolman, pointing to McKenney's white hair.

An officer is shown a photograph of a young Hispanic man he had arrested the night before for drug possession. "This guy hanged himself at Central Booking," he is told. "He's alive but he's brain dead."

The cop nods without comment.

O'Rourke and his squad gather outside in the parking lot, passing the incoming day tour. A few exchange high-fives, as they prepare for their evening's work.

A cop bends to touch his toes; his joints creak. "Riding in a car for eight hours a day for ten years takes its toll. It's the knees, both of mine."

The gas gauge is broken in a patrol car. "So how do you tell how much gas you have?" Officer Pete Schmidt asks, annoyed.

"You don't," says Officer Robert Smith, his partner.

The front seat is broken, too, barely supported by a milk crate. "I just got one seat fixed. Now this one's broken," Schmidt says. "And the arm is missing." He pulls down the front seat and looks at the backseat. "Slobs! They're animals, animals!" he grumbles, tossing out newspapers, Snapple bottles, and food wrappers.

These cops on the four-to-twelve tour are edgier, older, and more cynical than their morning and midnight counterparts. It takes a few hours for the mornings to heat up and then for the midnights to cool down. But on this shift the radio is often busy and the cops know they can expect almost anything before the shift is over. Most have steady partners, a few do not. Rookies move uneasily among the crowd.

Rookies used to be shunned by their older counterparts, standing on a footpost, waiting to be accepted by their older peers, and then finally partnering up with an older veteran for the prestige of riding in a patrol car. Pairing veterans and rookies was first stopped in 1972 by the Knapp Commission, on the theory that rookies would be tainted by the habits and temperament of veterans and thus more prone to corruption. Now, two partners with four years between them ride together.

"If I ride with a rookie and he's driving," says a veteran cop, "we'll go all around the precinct in four and a half minutes. Where do you go from there?"

The New York City Health Department has reported that East Harlem was the third most likely place in the city you would be stabbed, the second most likely place you'd be assaulted. Men, the agency reported, were more than three times more likely than women to be in harm's way. Teenagers were twice as likely to be a victim of a crime here than anywhere else in the city.

The four-to-midnight tour of the 23rd Precinct walks and rolls out into the square mile that they will patrol for the next eight hours: six cops in three cars, six on footposts.

East Harlem changes in the afternoon. Schools begin dismissing students, many of whom live in the neighborhood. Others crowd buses and subways on their way home to other boroughs. The youngest are met, without fail, by mothers or older relatives waiting patiently outside their schools.

Older teenagers hang around, boys gathering on corners with boom boxes; girls model up and down Third Avenue for them. Some teenagers head home to their own children. The more determined take up their notebooks and textbooks. The smell of marijuana from blunts—hollowed out cigars filled with marijuana—drifts through the air.

Junkies and drug dealers rise and filter through the streets, having awakened after their late forays of the night before. They set up business once again.

"I hate this post," Officer Nathan Martin complains. "It's got to be the fuckin' worst. It's dead. So fuckin' boring out here today, they should let us all go home early."

"They've got to get an electronics shop so you can sit down and watch TV," his partner says.

Officers David Laredo and Martin watch a man they suspect is selling drugs walk into a building. "It's a game. It's his job to run away. Your job is to catch him. He's stupid. He'll be back in the same spot," Martin predicted. "If everything was the way it should be, we wouldn't need cops. One-ten and Lex—this is the toilet of the world."

One Hundred and Tenth Street and Lexington Avenue looks like the crossroads between hell and salvation. It is usually staffed on day and evening shifts by at least two cops from the precinct. These rookies man their footposts by standing inside of bodegas to brace themselves against cold and rain, and the heat of the summer, leaning on buildings, and walking back and forth in a one block radius. A large cross-section of the neighborhood passes through on the way to the subway station to catch the Number 6 train at Lexington Avenue. Junkies, teeth missing, their limbs moving in a herky-jerky motion, lifeless, eyes staring, carrying the sweet/sour smell of too few baths, hands plump from too many needles, are called "skells." Potential or probable criminals are called "mopes."

A young man in a Yankees cap and Tommy Hilfiger denim shirt asks for directions to the precinct. "When you ask someone where they live, they tell you, 'Over there,' " said Officer Laredo to his partner, turning his back. "Tell him, 'Over there.' "

At one of the three bodegas, a woman dressed in her Sunday best topped by a black hat with a huge purple flower, had con-

cluded her prayers in church and stepped into a bodega for some
much needed libation. She purchased two bottles of Colt 40 and
a package of cigarettes before continuing her journey, spitting on
the ground as she glared at the two cops looking at her.

"You are a piece of shit to them," Laredo said. "They want you
to know that you're a public servant. You're just a schmuck with
a badge."

"Where are you guys off to?" Officer Martin asks a patrol car
that has stopped at the light.

"Constantly patrolling, as per the Academy," the driver answers. "We're the roving eyes and ears of the Department."

A black man, a little older than a teenager, raises his hand in
a black power salute and yells, "Fuck the police!" as he walks
down into the train station.

"There are no good-looking girls here," Laredo complains.
"Someone said there's a lot of hot-looking girls."

Officer Smith walks through his beat, writing summonses for beer
drinking, public urination, boxes of bullets, expired vehicle reg-
istrations, double-parked cars. His neatly pressed uniform and hat
can be seen a block away and as he is spotted, buyers and sellers
disperse, convening again when he is out of sight. Smith looks
around warily. One day, walking through 110th Street and Lexington Avenue, he heard gunshots. Two men were shooting at each
other, thirteen rounds in all, just as Smith landed on the corner.
He stopped one man.

"I said, 'You move, I'll blow your fuckin' head off.' He had a
loaded thirty-eight. He was probably trying to shoot back. Me?
Scared? There was no time to get scared. It lasted for about five
seconds."

He walks through 109th and Madison Avenue, looking away
from the hatred in the eyes of two dark-skinned Hispanic men
who never blink, following Smith's every movement. Smith was

once attacked by a drug dealer who smashed him over the head with a pipe for interfering on his turf. The drug dealer was tackled, restrained, handcuffed, arrested, and released from jail all in one day.

Smith enters a five-floor tenement building on the north side of the street, next to a vacant lot. Its front door is unlocked and propped open with a brick. He sticks his hand inside of empty mailboxes, looking for packages of drugs, and runs his hand over the door ledge. He walks up the stairs, human feces and a pool of urine greeting him at the top landing, and goes onto the roof. He nudges crack pipes, hypodermic needles, and bottle caps with his boots and looks over at the tranquillity of Central Park.

"It's pretty much of a theater, isn't it?"

At the opposite end of the precinct, Officer Mike Fields is on his footpost from 102nd to 105th Street, Third Avenue to the FDR Drive on the East River. He stands across from Park East High School against a background of abandoned and burnt-out buildings.

"This place is booby trapped," he says, pointing to a boarded-up structure. "It's not safe for us to go in there. There's nothing salvageable about this building. The stairs are missing, the fire escape fell down. This block is a problem," he says as he turned in a slow circle. "The smoke shops sell marijuana. They're dealing in front of the ninety-nine-cent store. That guy is a drug dealer over there." He points to a young Hispanic man wearing an Afro. "He's a manager. He doesn't carry stuff, he just directs people. I'm out here every day. I know what goes on."

"This is a strange place for a school," he says. "Most of these kids hate cops. I did, too, when I was younger," Fields admits. "I try and change that. Some will come up and say, 'How you doin', officer'? They'll say you're different. It's important for cops to communicate with everyone.

"How you doing?" he says to a group of guys sitting in front of the boarded-up store. "They used to sell out of here, sell mari-juana. The landlord loses money on rent. Nobody came here to buy sneakers. A lot of places don't sell anymore." He waves to Officer Dave LaGuardia.

LaGuardia often stops in at a smaller satellite school (now closed) on 108th and Second Avenue, and checks in with the principal at least once a day. Fifteen students had been suspended during the month of May, including a girl who arrived drunk, dropped her pants, and urinated on the floor. Three others were suspended for cutting classes, two for kicking in the classroom door, and one girl for being verbally abusive and hitting her teacher.

"When I got on the job, I thought I'd like to help people. Seventy percent is the opposite of what I thought. You have to do what the Police Department tells you to do. You have to stand on the street corner and you're not allowed to move. How can you help people? I'm paid not to think, the zombie phase."

"It was a culture shock," he said of East Harlem. "The way they lived, the way they acted, the way they accepted certain things. You hear about fifteen-year-old kids who have babies and you see it every day. People who don't want to get jobs, people on public assistance—the ones that take advantage of it—you see it every day. Sometimes with a job like mine, you have to put attitude aside. You can't condemn everybody. You can't stereotype everybody."

Officer Paul Lawson shares his patrol car with Officer Guillermo Hernandez, a quiet, almost shy man, a counterpart to Lawson's jocularity and philosophical bent. Lawson is short, dark-haired, and midwestern—pleasant. He is small and muscular. His taller partner, light-skinned with a wandering mustache, wears his light-brown hair short and always looks immaculate.

"I thought he was deaf and mute. I thought he would be the

perfect partner because I talk a lot," Lawson jokes as they turn a corner.

"This is the only neighborhood where a beer bottle is a musical instrument," he says, as he watches a man blow into the neck of the bottle. Two men bang on conga drums accompanied by a pair of women performing a drunken dance in a playground. "Must be the rum kickin' in. Some people get four summonses in one week," he says. "They don't care."

They waved to Sergeant O'Rourke and his driver, Walter McKenney, who are supervising them during the evening. "I was looking for someone who spoke Spanish and acted their age, so I picked Gil. Before that I used to work with Anita Perez. She didn't question what I did and I didn't question what she did. You will have a high percentage of women who will wimp out. You have to fight. You have to be strong enough until the cavalry comes. Sometimes it's not even a matter of being strong. They're street kids who can punch you out. They've been fighting all their lives. If you wimp out, there's no return. If you don't fight to the death, someone will know about it. I'd be lying to tell you that I'm not afraid. But no one wants to talk about it because then we have to face it."

At 110th Street and Lexington Avenue, bodegas occupy three corners, while the fourth is edged by a fenced-in housing development. The Aguilar Branch of the New York Public Library is down the block. Lawson waves to the foot patrolmen and eyes a scrawny woman overdosing on makeup and alcohol. She staggers down the street.

"People who look like normal people, a few months later they look like a mess because of all the drug use. The amount of drugs, the amount of homeless people—people don't have much here. I feel sorry for people, you know, who are working to improve themselves. But I don't feel sorry for drug addicts."

"Just because they live in this neighborhood doesn't mean they're bad people," Hernandez says quietly. "I grew up in a

neighborhood like this in Brooklyn. I remember the humiliation
of being in the subway and being approached. I know what to look
for, and when I see people, I know where they're going. That's the
rule of the ghetto. If you run from a cop, you're disrespecting him
and you'll get a beating."

"*Two-three, David,*" the voice of the dispatcher calls over the
radio.

"David," Hernandez replies.

East Harlem, like every neighborhood in New York City, is
broken up into small territories by the alphabet. Lawson and Hernandez patrolled the E sector: Eddie, in police jargon. A was
Adam; B, Boy; C, Charlie; D, David.

Two sisters, both black women in their mid-twenties, wearing
old jeans and dirty coats, were demanding money. They had
staked out their territory: 96th to 100th Streets, from Fifth and
Madison Avenues, where they were preying on elderly women,
yelling and intimidating them into handing over a few cents, a few
dollars. Lawson and Hernandez pull their patrol car to the corner
of Madison and 98th Street, stop and observe the two women who
are so busy they don't notice the patrol car. One of the women is
pregnant. She intercepts an elderly white woman with a cane and
blocks her from moving.

"That's it," Lawson says firmly, as he and Hernandez step
quickly out of the car. They approach the black woman and ask
for identification. Her sister waits across the street. The elderly
accosted woman, who looks to be about eighty, interrupts, lifting
up her cane and pointing it at Lawson.

"Why, do you know who I am? You won't be working here for
long," she warns.

Lawson opens his mouth to say something but then decides
against it. He writes out a summons for disorderly conduct while
the black woman stands defiantly, with her hand on her hip, next
to the elderly woman clutching her cane.

"You can't win," he mutters as they walk back to the patrol car. Before he can turn the key in the ignition, the dispatcher radios them again. Heart attack.

Lawson and Hernandez siren away. They arrive before the paramedics at a high rise on First Avenue, unsure if they will be performing CPR or if the person is dead. Would she be surrounded by heartbroken relatives or angry ones? Was it really a heart attack? Could it be murder, or would it be a mundane stop?

They knock on the door of apartment 14D quickly, calling out, "Police!"

A young black woman in a neatly pressed T-shirt and jeans opens the door, behind her a picture window with a view of the East River and the twinkling lights of New York City and its bridges. Paramedics arrive, breathlessly rushing by her as a little boy runs around naked, squealing and jumping up and down on a white couch.

"I'm not feeling well," she says, gold bracelets dangling and wiping her nose with her hand. They open a stretcher. "So I called 911 and said I was having a heart attack. I think I have a little cold."

Lawson and Hernandez look at each other and roll their eyes. She turns to check on her son. They turn the case over to the paramedics.

"They use it as a taxi service," Lawson complains. "It's cheaper. In the meantime, the paramedics could be handling something more serious."

Another young woman, Hispanic, calls the 911 emergency number, needing aspirin for her baby.

"The call probably came in saying someone was unconscious. If she had checked with an adult or a family physician, it would have been different," Lawson says. He felt the girl's forehead and checked her pulse. "The flu's going around," he tells her. "I have a little girl, too, who's eleven months and she's had the flu." The entire family—mother, grandmother, and two children—ride in the ambulance with the paramedics who take them to the emergency room at Metropolitan Hospital five blocks away.

The dispatcher radios for sector Adam; a woman has reported that her boyfriend is hitting her.

"Eddie on the back," Officer Hernandez advises, letting the dispatcher know that he and Officer Lawson would back them up, along with Sergeant O'Rourke. A call for domestic violence means that someone will have to be arrested and, in an unpredictable situation where emotions replace reason, cops could become the target.

They enter a dark apartment, a young Hispanic man in jeans and a sweatshirt letting them in. A woman points him out.

"He hit me."

"Fuckin' goddamn bitch! No, I didn't."

"Guy! Guy! Calm down," someone calls out.

The man reluctantly allows himself to be handcuffed. He is to go down the stairs, into the patrol car, and then have his business sorted out at the precinct house. He refuses to walk down the stairs, twisting his torso back and forth and pushing against the cop who holds him. Two cops push him forward. A man and a woman watch through an apartment door, run out and jump on one of the cops, who pushes them away.

"You're beating him down!" they insist.

"Hey, we're not beating him down," the cop says to them, finally arriving at the first floor.

Officers Lawson and Hernandez look up at the roof and help hustle the man into sector Adam's patrol car. They climb back into their own. The backseat is neat, clean, and organized: two hats, two memo books, two nightsticks side by side. Each time they left their patrol, each partner would grab his hat and place it squarely on his head; not wearing it would be a violation of the Patrol Guide.

Headquarters wants them in uniform and looking like cops. A bottle, thrown from the building, shatters against the sidewalk.

Officer Lawson, the son of a minister, doesn't wear his bulletproof vest. "I'm in God's hands," he says. "The vest is uncomfortable. If I'm going to get shot, it's not in man's hands. Not that God allows people to get shot. He allows things to happen. If I'm supposed to die or get shot, I have a lot of sympathy for the person who shoots me."

Hernandez looks at him in surprise. "I'm wearing *mine*," he says. "If you get a guy up against a wall, you're scared."

"Some are like Gil," Lawson said of his partner. "He's not scared. He knows what to expect. If you're an average guy living in the suburbs and coming here, you're scared. If they say not, they're lying. You don't think about the scary part."

The police radio was a little quieter. A rock thrown at the patrol car narrowly missed the windshield and bounced onto Lexington Avenue.

"I prefer working in a Spanish area rather than a black area," Lawson said. "Spanish respect you more and people like you more. Spanish people are better. But when they're drinking, they'll fight you, especially in front of a woman. A lot of times you speak to someone that's black and they give you that attitude. People try to show off in front of the crowd. It just gets really bad. People try and turn on you, calling you a racist, a liar. You get verbally abused. You can take so much before you snap. The minute someone pushes you, that's it. They can say all the want. If they physically touch you, they've got to go. If the police told me to leave, I would leave. You lock people up, and you're called racist."

A team of rookies sails through a red light, no lights, no sirens. "I have a family. You think I'm barreling through lights?" Lawson says.

He looks at the crowds of teenagers on 109th and Madison and dotting Third Avenue as they drive around. "I don't call them African Americans," Lawson says of the people he arrests. "I call them niggers. They're up to no good. African Americans are working, trying to make it better for themselves.

"You don't know who's your enemy and who's your friend. It's not like wearing a uniform and yours is black and theirs is gray. You would be surprised at how many people you smile at and they turn away. You can't police the streets the way the law is written. There's never a perfect arrest," he says. "By law, you can't move them off a corner. You have to be able to get them off that fuckin' corner. These are all nonconformists to society's understanding. You've got to be able to say, 'Listen, get the fuck out of here.' Civilians say, 'That's too rough.' That's why it's frustrating. People forget who we're being mean to. You're being mean to someone else who's making someone else's life miserable.

"Some of the people we're talking to, they deserve to be told, 'Bitch, shut up.' That's the only language they understand. You get a lot of bullshit complaints.

"The cops are losing their power. The cops are getting fed up with not being backed by society. Society has to back up the police. Well, submit an alternative. There is no alternative. When you're a rookie, you think about work every day. I don't think about this job whatsoever when I go home. You look at it as a job. I think every day there's a frustration. When you see some people standing on the corner, you know they're dealing drugs and you can't do anything about it.

"The guidelines keep expanding or shrinking. When I step out of the car, there are so many guidelines, I don't want to step out of the car. You step out of a car and a guy tells you to fuck yourself. 'I don't have to tell you shit. Go to hell.' What about *your* freedom of speech? We have none. He can curse and there's nothing you can do.

"This is a good job. Everyone is proud to be a cop. They know that you can be called to test your own bravery and heroism. It's kind of ironic that society puts us here to protect everyone and they hate us. They don't treat people with respect. Everyone wants to be a cop. You come here and you're a dick."

"*Two-three, Boy,*" the radio dispatcher announces, "*man with a gun, black male, five feet seven inches tall, approximately forty years old, plaid jacket...*" The dispatcher spoke quickly.

Officer Steven Flanagan turns a corner and they spot him almost immediately. John Palmetto and Flanagan speed to the curb, braking sharply as two other patrol cars pull up behind them. Flanagan jumps out. He grabs a .357 magnum from the man's waistband, and empties it of bullets.

Since the dispatcher has called for another sector car to handle the job, Palmetto and Flanagan give the arrest to Officer Anita Perez and her partner, who were just a step behind them when they encountered the gunman.

"I would never suspect an old black man of carrying a gun unless he was a Southerner," Perez says, the only female cop on the scene. "He was forty-seven, forty-eight. He said that a kid had taken his ten dollars and that he was getting even. This guy was a seasoned criminal. He was an old-timer. He was going to buy dope or coke. He confessed to shooting a guy in the arm."

"I look forward to work every day," Flanagan says. "Some days it's dead, some days real busy. There's always something new. You get paid to experience life. I like running around. I love coming to work and getting involved in things. You have the best seats. You're right there. I love this job. I love riding around in a sector car. I love standing on the corner watching people go by. Gun collars are the greatest. You always know there's one less gun."

Officer Palmetto has black hair neatly trimmed and so wavy and shiny it looks like icing. Flanagan is a thin man wearing circular framed eyeglasses and has the quiet demeanor of a priest. He is four years older than his partner, who is also in his twenties. He attended Holy Cross University in Worcester, Massachusetts, majoring, he says, in Grateful Dead concerts with a minor in philosophy.

Back on patrol, they stop their car at 109th and Madison Avenue. Black and Hispanic teenage boys, with pit bulls, police the block, counting wads of cash like old businessmen.

After circling around the precinct, the patrol car is littered with empty Chinese takeout cartons and soy sauce packets. They answer a radio call for a dispute at a bar across the street from the precinct house. Through the open door, Officers Frank Torrellas and Jimmy Russo could see a man dressed in construction clothing seated on a barstool, his face leaning flat against the bar. The owner, mustache shaking, is waving his arms. The customer won't or can't move and hasn't paid his tab.

"Hello! Hello!" Russo shouts at the inert customer.

The man looks up blankly, his dark hair stuck to his face, so drunk he can barely lift his head.

"You have to pay your bar tab!" Russo yells again.

"Whaaa?" The customer's head rolls around, his eyes unfocused.

"I want my money," the owner demands.

"How much does he owe you?" Russo asks.

"Nineteen dollars."

"You have to pay him," Russo announces. "You have to pay him!"

The man shakes his head and then rests it back down on the bar.

"I want him arrested!" the owner says.

Russo sighs. "We're not supposed to do this but . . ." he says

to himself, putting his hand into the man's back pocket and removing his wallet. He counts out nineteen dollars.

"This is the simplest way to end the dispute," he says.

The owner, satisfied, lets the man sleep.

Two sons, grown men, are pummeling each other in the living
room of their small apartment; their mother calls 911 to report a
fight. The mother holds on to one son, blood dripping down his
face, his shirt torn. The other son, glassy-eyed, leans against a
wall, breathing heavily.

"What's up, guys?" asks Officer Lawson.

The mother insists that her son, leaning against the wall,
stabbed his brother with a knife.

The two brothers suddenly charge each other. Lawson and Hernandez pry them apart. The mother runs after the uninjured son.

"He must be high on something," Hernandez notes.

The mother says she doesn't want anyone arrested. Not finding
a knife, the two cops let the family settle the argument themselves.

Back in their sector car, they turn a corner and drive into the
final round of a fight that had begun at a White Castle. Four patrol
cars surround the restaurant. Lawson and Hernandez piece the
story together. Two teenagers had brushed against each other
while waiting on line for their wafer-thin hamburgers. They moved
their argument into the street where the "cousin" of one stabbed
the other. Gang beads lie in a pool of blood in the gutter.

"Yo, he bumped him. That ain't right," says the stabber. "He
started fuckin' with me 'cause he thought I thought he was nothin'.
That's my blood, man, my blood."

"Everyone is a cousin," says Lawson, getting back into the patrol car as another sector car handles the arrest. The radio was
busy. "You never know what to expect," he sighs.

"Oh, yes, we do," replies his partner, his arm hanging out the
window.

*   *   *

A middle-aged Hispanic man wearing a plaid flannel shirt and blue jeans, urinates against the side of an apartment building. Officer Palmetto slams on the brakes, causing his partner's hat to topple off.

"You think you can take a piss wherever you want?" he calls out to the offender, who hurriedly zips his pants.

"Go stand on the corner," Palmetto orders. "Hold out your driver's license and stand by the telephone."

Palmetto follows, squinting to read. He writes down the man's name and address in his summons book, refusing to touch the license. "Peeing against the wall," Palmetto says, shaking his head.

He hands back the summons. "Read the back of the summons," he says. "Go to court but urinate no more."

"Two-three, Adam."

The dispatcher calls out to them; a woman living in the projects has called 911 to report that her upstairs neighbor is pouring ammonia down the plumbing pipes.

"How could she know that?" Flanagan asks, dumbfounded.

Arriving at her apartment, they ring the bell and rap on the door with their nightsticks. No answer. Turning away, two Housing cops approach.

"It's a mentally disturbed woman who calls repeatedly," they inform Palmetto and Flanagan, who conclude the call.

Driving back to the stationhouse, they stroll to the men's room as two Chinese men wearing identical dirty white aprons speak with Detective Bryan Lorenzo of the robbery unit. One says he was beaten and robbed by twenty-five black and Hispanic teenagers while riding through Jefferson Park to make a delivery. They punched him and stole his bicycle. The second man works at a nearby restaurant.

Palmetto and Flanagan listen carefully as he translates. Detective Lorenzo radios the dispatcher to report the crime and the description of the perpetrators. The delivery man rides with Palmetto and Flanagan as cops, on foot and in patrol cars, fan out through Jefferson Park.

"Central, we have a possible!" comes a chorus of voices. In the shadows by a fence, a group of teenagers mills around. Spotted, they split up, running in twos and threes in different directions. Palmetto and Flanagan cut them off by the FDR Drive, their patrol car angled against a fence. The delivery man excitedly points out three. Two are thirteen-year-old twins, the other is fifteen.

"It wasn't us," they protest, even though the details of the crime have yet to be revealed. "We weren't there. Who you talkin' about? We ain't there, man."

The two are stuffed in one car, the third in another, and delivered to the robbery unit detective who will investigate. But all the delivery man wanted was his bicycle back.

"This isn't going to go anywhere," predicts Detective Lorenzo. "The Asians do not press charges."

An older Puerto Rican man in a tattered jacket approaches their car and taps on the window. Officer Russo rolls it down halfway as the man sticks his face in the car. "Trees are on fire," he warns, pointing to the corner, and then continues on down the block.

Russo pulls the car up slowly so their food won't spill. There are no trees on the corner.

"Anything burning?" Russo asks his partner, sniffing the air. "No? Let's eat!"

Torrellas peels an orange. Because of his diabetes, he injects himself with insulin daily and eats at least five small meals a day. "To me, it's my life. I've got to eat regularly. I don't get any special treatment," he said. "If I feel sick, I call in. It bothers me a lot to do that. With Jimmy, he knows my situation." A banana rests inside of his hat on the back seat. Music is blaring from an apartment window.

"Do you need speakers as large as a refrigerator?" Russo asks.

"Why does your neighbor upstairs, downstairs and across the street have to hear it? It's almost like a status thing."

"In the Two-three, these people are more realistic to me," Torrellas says, throwing peels over his shoulder and onto the backseat. "I grew up in this kind of neighborhood. You're dealing with well-educated people in the Nineteenth Precinct and not well-educated here. It's the haves and the have-nots. You have people living here at the poverty level and just above. People living from paycheck to paycheck, kids eighteen years old driving a Porsche, drug dealers. . . . Kids here, they bought their cars with cash. Daddy didn't buy it."

"Eye for eye, tooth for tooth, hairpiece for hairpiece," says Russo.

Finishing their meal, they start up again.

Rounding corners, they find themselves on Fifth Avenue, heading south along Central Park. Russo pulls over.

"Look! There's a cottontail rabbit!" he cries out, pointing out a fast brown rabbit to his unimpressed partner.

"Dinner!" Torrellas proclaims with gusto.

They turn onto 109th and Madison, slowing down to eyeball teenagers standing around, eyeballing them, their pants slung low—gold teeth and dead eyes. Russo keys the loudspeaker.

"Ahem! Ahem!" he says, clearing his throat into the microphone. *"Good night!"* he waves.

They move.

Turning onto East 108th Street, the dispatcher alerts them to an electrical fire on the fourth floor of a tenement building in the middle of the block. Lights in the entranceway flicker on and off. Russo and Torrellas walk up four floors, the smoke thickening the closer they come to the apartment. Black smoke filters from the door and windows. Torrellas strolls into the apartment, looking for its occupants, leaving his worried partner behind in the hallway.

"Frank! Frank!" Russo calls nervously. "Where is he?!"

There is no answer. Firemen begin ushering people out of apartments as hall lights blink.

"Oh, God! Frank!" groans Russo, taking a deep breath, and plunging into the dense smoke. A few minutes later, both men emerge, coughing, as firemen enter the apartment.

They stand out in the pouring rain. "What are you trying to do to me?" Russo says to Torrellas angrily, but with concern. "If you want to be a fuckin' fireman, be a fuckin' fireman!"

A fireman punches out windows. A resident complains loudly about being inconvenienced. "The building's got illegal wiring with violations," says a fire official.

Torrellas complains of feeling lightheaded and of a tightness in his chest.

"Central, put us out at Metropolitan Hospital," Russo says quickly, driving to the Emergency Room.

A nurse hooks them up to oxygen, both men breathing deeply into the plastic masks.

"Hey, this is the planet of the apes!" jokes Russo, removing his uniform shirt and bulletproof vest. Underneath is a white T-shirt with the sleeves ripped off, a small rip just underneath the V-neck.

"Hey, didn't your mother tell you to put on clean underwear?" says Torrellas, eyeing his partner's physique. "Hey, look at those breasts!" he exclaims, squeezing Russo's chest and then pinching the roll ringing his partner's waist. "Hey, let's crank up the oxygen!"

Finally, the two partners are silent. Russo's father was a cop. Half of Torrellas's family are cops: brothers, cousins, uncles.

Russo removes his oxygen mask first and checks on his partner.

"Frank, are you still with us?" he asks. Torrellas closes his eyes, pretending not to hear. "Frank!"

Torrellas strips off his oxygen mask and the two men put their bulletproof vests and uniform shirts back on. "Ah, paradise," Torrellas sighs. "Let's get the hell out of here."

By the Book

Five p.m. was the middle of the day for Captain Matt Carmody, the executive officer at the 23rd Precinct, who often worked double shifts to accommodate the schedule that his wife worked. He sits behind the green metal desk, paperwork piled up, as he reads stock reports. He is a former Vietnam vet, UPS driver, and reformed alcoholic. He peers through the blinds of his office, spotting two female summons cops, one black and one Hispanic, standing on the corner chatting.

"What the fuck are they doing?" he asks, annoyed. "They haven't moved in the last hour. The last time I complained, they called me a fuckin' racist. Oh, I hate this fuckin' place." He sighs.

The phone rings; it is his wife checking in, letting him know that their two young children, sick with colds, were doing better. His first wife, the daughter of a PBA honcho, had remarried an indicted and disbarred PBA lawyer who still maintains ties to the police union. Somewhere in the scheme of things, Carmody feels these two men still exert influence.

He had injured his wrist in a notorious incident at a Harlem mosque where a police radio and gun were stolen. He kept appearing before police doctors who told him there was nothing wrong with his hand. He couldn't hold a pen or a fork in the injured hand, so he taught himself how to write left-handed, and then developed carpal tunnel syndrome. "I want to get the fuck out of here. The job is driving me fuckin' crazy," he says, eating frozen burritos that have thawed out in the bottom drawer of his desk. Dousing them with Tabasco sauce, he peels back the wrapper and eats them, using *Barron's* magazine as his placemat. "What's with these fuckin' people anyway? These people need supervision. Yesterday, everyone was in the stationhouse, thirty-five minutes over meal. No one was out on patrol. Community Policing comes in for a meal and stays for two hours," he complains. "This is not the paramilitary. This is the Cub Scouts."

Captain Carmody's responsibilities included supervising lieutenants, sergeants, and cops, handling complaints and reviewing paperwork. Like every other captain, he took a civil service test as he made his way up through the ranks and was assigned to different precincts throughout Manhattan by the New York City Police Department. Because of his injury, he wore a suit and tie, didn't carry a gun, which he couldn't shoot anyway, and was confined to the stationhouse. At the age of forty-two, with straight, graying hair, he left his door open to cops and other visitors, answered the phone on the first ring, and kept the television turned to the British comedy *Absolutely Fabulous*.

"Nobody has any common sense," he says, wiping stray crumbs

off the desk with a paper towel. "This is a microcosm. Every precinct does things a certain way. Everyone likes to think that their precinct is unique. Everyone likes to say that they're slaves to the radio," he complains. "But no one picks up jobs when they're on a footpost. The beat cops do not pick up jobs on the radio. They do whatever the fuck they want. The sectors do whatever they want. There's no consistency. People don't even know how to fill out a complaint form."

After Captain Robert Curley's two year term was up and he was moved to headquarters, Executive Officer Carmody had to adjust to the styles and whims of the next three commanding officers, often acting as a buffer between cops and the captain.

"Every day you're going to be connected with a set of circumstances. You don't want to look like you don't know what you're doing. You don't have the resources to feel confident to make decisions. But make it look like you have control. In a crisis, you'll feel like there's someone in charge. The New York City Police Department is a quasi-paramilitary organization. You don't have any choice. You're given an assignment. You have to make it work.

"There is a difference between errors of the heart and errors of the mind. There's a difference between a guy not knowing a procedure and making an omission, and just not properly carrying out an assignment and willfully circumventing the procedures. That's how you have to deal with it—was it an honest mistake or someone playing games? One of the best things would be to teach cops about their heritage on this job, and how it evolved. I think that everyone should have a sense of history, a little more pride in the Department. If I went to take a job on the outside, I'd better know a little about the company. A lot of men and women came before us. The job gives a lot of silly courses on how to recognize signs of police who are at risk. It doesn't take an idiot to see who's at risk. There's a lot of perceived pressure from this job, whether it's actually there or not. I don't think they've done enough to alleviate internal pressure. Guys still have a high suspicion of inner workings on the job, worrying about covering your back, your ass, for being second-guessed, and disciplinary action."

Just over two hundred cops are under his domain: rookies, veterans, those looking to move on, move up, or move out.

The captains and the commanding officer, for the most part, have no input or control over who works of their precinct, from rookies and cops considered problems elsewhere, to others who are solid and hard-working, with immaculate records. Once a year or so, cops are informally rotated by promotion, assigned to other units, or they retire. The average age at the 23rd Precinct is twenty-five.

Not all cops make arrests. "Only ten percent of cops are making arrests," explains Carmody. "Ninety percent do other things, like writing summonses. This Department for years discouraged you from making arrests," he says. "I went to roll call and they never talked about crime. 'Summonses are down. Stay out of this area because it's corrupt. If you're seen at this place, you'll get a complaint.' There are things that used to be shoved down our throats. I worked in the Three-two. I never heard, 'Listen, we have a pattern of robberies.' Never did they touch on that. Then, you go out there. There could have been two homicides on the tour before and it was never an issue. Arrests generated overtime and they did not want you to make overtime. It was dollars and cents."

At the 23rd Precinct on the day tour, one team was known to start with a cup of coffee and a newspaper, parking their patrol car by the Lexington Avenue bus depot, no matter how busy the precinct was. A team on the four-to-twelve was documented by the Inspections Unit as failing to answer jobs. Reprimanded and punished by the captain, they blamed the captain.

"You're never going to know," Captain Carmody says of the character of cops, "until you get in the car as a cop. I don't think that there are any thieves here or any hooked on drugs. A few drunks," he says. "It's perpetual high school."

One particular cop, assigned to stationhouse security, would disappear. Another team let Central know that they were responding to a job, but stopped and got coffee or a sandwich first. A few cops identified the cooping locations and used them.

"How many [jobs] are going to offer you twenty years and a pension and [let you] retire at forty? The least you can do is work," one cop suggests. Some cops, fearful of making the wrong decision, don't make any decision. "People won't take the initiative. They're not sure of themselves. They never answer up. They're never there. You just hope that they're wearing the vest and see the bullet coming."

It's the law of averages. The more a police officer does, the more likely he is to get involved in something.

"They have all these crazy rules about lethal force, 'What would a rational person . . .' Goddamn it, who's rational?" asks Sergeant Columbo. "We speed to gunfire. I'm out of my fuckin' mind—a rational person will go home. You're there. If I'm on the street, now, I'm glad to see [fellow officer] Victorio Roma show up. He can fight. He's got a bad-ass attitude. Would I want to go out drinking with him? Hell, no. I think he's a good guy. He was brought up a little differently. He was brought up believing that niggers and spics were bad. He fuckin' sees it. But he's an accident waiting to happen."

Officer Billy Valdez and his partner kick open the door to the roof on East 102nd Street. Although a 911 call had just come in for two pit bulls running loose on the roof without their owner, the brownstone's rooftop is quiet: no two- or four-legged creatures. Valdez loses sight of his partner for a moment.

"Oh, shit!" his partner exclaims, as a snarling, coiled pit bull jumps over the ledge separating the adjacent rooftops, and runs furiously toward him. He tries to push the dog away with his nightstick, lunges off balance, and falls. The dog sets to pounce, a shot rings out. The dog staggers back. Valdez has pulled his gun and fired, saving his partner from the deadly jaws of the pit bull. A second one races across the rooftop, snarling. A sergeant and another cop gun it down.

"Lucky that a child wasn't up there," Valdez says afterward. "It would have been ripped to shreds by those two dogs."

After the pit bulls are carted off, their owner receives several summonses. Valdez looks at the rooftop itself. Ten bullets have made identical, small, round holes in the tarpaper. He descends the stairs, warily. The shots have penetrated the roof, leaving ten identical small, round holes in the ceiling and walls.

"Holy shit!" He is horrified. "Imagine if someone were standing there."

He knocks on apartment doors to be certain that no bullets have hit any of its occupants. "Thank God!" he says, with a sigh of relief. "Can you imagine some poor guy sitting in the apartment and bullets are coming through? Thank God no one was hurt."

If Valdez had hesitated, his partner might have been maimed by the pit bull. But what if someone had been injured or—worse— killed by an errant bullet? If Valdez had followed a Police Department technique by taking his nightstick, bending down, and bracing it against the dog's neck, Valdez's face would be exposed to the lethal teeth of the squirming animal. Had anyone ever choked a pit bull before? A decision had to be made.

"I'm not going to judge anyone on this job," says Sergeant Kevin O'Rourke. "I'm not going to second guess you. It's not up to me. Sometimes things that are right for me are not right for someone else. He turns around and you shoot him. 'Oh, shit, it's not a knife. How are they going to react?' I don't think that upper management gives enough credit to cops and sergeants on the street to make a decision. You process information with whatever you see first. Why second guess someone? It's Monday morning quarterbacking."

When Tara Casey worked in Bushwick, Brooklyn, in the early 1970s, police justice, she says, was meted out with nightsticks. "We would take blacks to the cemetery where they were so spooked, they would confess."

Black cops, she says, demanded fear and respect out on the streets. "They were more feared by their own. In Harlem or Brooklyn, there were no holds barred. They beat the living life out of them [blacks]. White cops often called them off."

"There was rampant abuse through the eighties," says Detective Florio Romero of the 23rd Precinct. "A guy on my block drank beer and sat on the stoop. I lived on the fifth floor. I seen a cop car pull up and tell him to leave the stoop. That's his building! He tells the officer, 'I live here.' The beer can was inside of the bag. Then two cops grabbed him from where he was and brought him into a basement apartment. You could hear the shots on his head with a nightstick. It was like the sound of coconuts. They beat this guy and they left him. The Police Commissioner had to know. The abuse was rampant."

"I hated cops back then," says Detective Eddie Martinez. "I saw a lot of abuse. It was physical abuse by cops—blacks, Hispanics, whites. In the sixties, they tended to be more forceful to their own. I got slapped by a policeman once and boy, did it burn me. I took a tire valve off a car and used it as a whistle. Big, white Irish cop. I said, 'Never again will I get caught.' But I still did it. I was just more careful. It was an adversarial thing. It wasn't respect. It was fear, fear of the beating on you. Even back then, there was mistrust by that community, mostly blacks and Hispanics. Even back then, you didn't know what you can do. Could you drink a beer and lean up against a car? No matter what you were doing, they could slap you down. Everyone would stop and watch for the car even if they were just shooting marbles or playing stoop ball. Now people hear certain information and they'll take it as gospel. They don't make any attempt to go and find out anything. They'll believe anything. Once word gets out that it's cops, see how much they embellish it."

"All cops have these plastic things," Housing Police Lieutenant Johnny Broderick says, referring to nightsticks. "Years ago, you got a wooden nightstick. They were made of a hard wood called cocobola. Guys used to carry ax handles. They don't have a tendency to split. But they look too much like a club. Until 1984, you carried a blackjack or a slapper. If you used it, you had to justify it. A blackjack has a spring in the handle. It'll spring back and hit you again. You had head wounds; it was bloody, it was messy. If an officer is fighting by himself and he opens the guy's head up, it's much more understood. Each situation is different. The most difficult thing is to get handcuffs on someone when they don't want handcuffs on. They wrestle around, trying not to get their hands behind their back. There's no fear of authority."

"Man with a gun, One-oh-five and Second Avenue," the dispatcher interrupts.

Young black men with gold teeth stand in front of a vegetable stand, dealing drugs every day; cops say the owner is frightened of reprisals from local drug dealers if he calls the police. As cops approach, a black car pulls up to the curb. Two alleged drug dealers walk toward the car; one fits the description broadcast over the radio.

Did the man have a gun? Where was it? Was it loaded? Would he use it? Who would he shoot first? Who called 911? Was the caller a rival drug dealer harassing his competition?

Officer John Jackson, his hands on his holster, firmly orders the man to put his hands up in the air, a seemingly simple request. The man ignores him, his teeth and eyes gleaming. Jackson orders him again, and again he refuses. Jackson and his partner grab his hands before he can get at his gun. The man pushes them away, punching and kicking. Four more cops show up and they wrestle him to the ground, finally handcuffing him. Still, he kicks and clubs with his elbows. Thirty, forty people gather around, including a woman in a fur coat who jumps out of a cab shouting, "You can't do this!"

Cops lift the man to his feet and push him into a patrol car. He curses at them, "Goddamn motherfuckers!" Sitting inside the patrol car, his face a mask of hate, he riles the crowd of black and Hispanic teenagers taunting the cops, and kicks the back of the seats.

"Po-lice brutality!" the crowd calls out. "He ain't done nothing!"

As soon as the cops and the man they have arrested arrive in the stationhouse, he suddenly becomes very quiet. "That was a show," explains one cop. "If the crowd wasn't there, it would have been a lot different."

The man, it turns out, didn't have a gun.

My partner and I used to go on family disputes," recalls Detective Eduardo Fernandez who patrolled in East Harlem during the seventies and eighties. "We said, 'If we have to come back here we're going to make sure you're going to jail and you don't come back. Another call, you're going to have a problem.' We wouldn't get another domestic violence call from that apartment. Back then and there, you'd grab the scruff of some kid's neck, take him ten blocks away in the patrol car, and you'd straighten him out. You wouldn't hear from that particular location anymore. You would take him and read him the riot act. There were times when you would find this woman with a shiner. 'You can't arrest him, I need him, I have three kids.' She would take it because she needed it. You caused him a little bit of pain. Nothing that was going to disable him. We would bring him back or leave him in a particular location. If it was a verbal dispute, strong language would keep him from doing it again. If she was battered, we would give him a good beating.

"Back then, a lot of cases were adjudicated out on the streets. You didn't have a complainant, so you didn't have a case. You didn't bring it back to the stationhouse. We would say, 'We don't want to come back here.' No jobs came back to that location for the remainder of the week. We'd go back and see if everything was okay. Sometimes it would take a little intervention and potentially a beating. At some point, the man had to be made aware that physically he could be hurt, too. 'If I did this to so and so, they could do this to me.' "

In sharp contrast, The New York City Police Department, under Commissioner Howard Safir, targeted domestic violence and made it mandatory to enforce orders of protection, to make an arrest, recommend counseling, track incidents, and make follow-up visits.

Although not all police condone brutality, a beating—called "a tuneup"—cops say, was once accepted as street justice. And people were fearful of complaining about them, afraid of repercussions whether they were innocent or guilty.

One cop carries questions about police brutality. An uncle of his from the Bronx was arrested and beaten to death by cops back in the mid-sixties.

"Six cops with nightsticks beat him to a pulp. He was driving a livery cab. It was a good case, but no one followed it up," recalls Detective Freddie Gonzalez. "Detectives went to the house a few times. His wife didn't pursue it because she had another lover. Her father and brother pursued it. The wife didn't really pay too much attention. People didn't want to start making waves. Who else can you turn to? My father's brother blamed the cops. I was scared to know what the answers were. I was scared to really know. How would I deal with it? It always comes to mind.

"Cops came to my house all the time. They were nasty. Once a month they had to throw my father out of the home. Fights? They were mean. They were always hitting and always pushing. My father was hitting my mother, so I didn't care if they hit him. It was pretty bad. They'd come back again. He wanted to instigate them. 'Kill me! You killed my brother!' he would tell them. He got arrested so many times.

"I always said that I could be working with the guy that killed my uncle. I used to see cops beating up people. I said, 'Damn! That could be my uncle.' "

Sergeant Charlie Columbo: "This job turns you into a racist. It depends on where you work. You tend to become much more leery of minorities. In Bensonhurst, I'm sure you're locking up Italians. Do cops trust cops? Overall, yes. Would I turn around and go to the district attorney and give up a cop? If he was dirty, yes, in a heartbeat.

"If you're stupid enough to try and take my gun, you're going to take a beating. If he's willing to fight a cop, he's going to kill him. I'm fighting for my fuckin' life. I have a gun and you're willing to fight me?! Are we supposed to get beat up? If I pull up to a fight and the guy is half dead and the cop is still beating him, I wouldn't say anything. But if you just smack a guy, I will take care of this. 'The next time that I see this I'm going to drop a dime and give them your name. You make us look like fuckin' animals.' Why hurt someone who doesn't deserve to be hit? You don't give out beatings to everyone. Some people need beatings. You're a cop. We deal with thirty percent of the public. What are we seeing? We're seeing victims, perps, people coming and going. Five to ten percent of the people are perps. Some are total assholes. They were brought up by animals. They were pissed, and to get back they fight. I'm going to kick the shit out of you. If you try and deal with them as a human, you're going to get hurt. The only thing they understand is violence.'"

"Are there people who deserve to be killed?" asks Sergeant Columbo. "Yes. For the fuckin' good of everybody."

On Madison Avenue, police question a long-time drug dealer. He runs, followed by two cops. A crowd gathers as two cops catch him and force his hands behind his back in order to handcuff him. A third cop stands in the background. The crowd is hostile, taunting them. Two women yell out, "Police brutality!" No one wants to know why he is being arrested, how many lives he has affected by dealing drugs, that he has punched a cop, run away, and resisted arrest. The neighborhood sees him as one of their own. "We're an enforcement unit. If I put my guard down, who knows what's going to happen?" says one cop. "It's better to be more cautious and get a fuckin' complaint."

"We had an individual down in police custody," recalls Detective Martinez. "He said the cop had a foot on his neck and choked him. Tons of people told us, 'Cops did it.' Calls were coming in like crazy. Cops did this; cops did that. The cops were taken off the street. You do the extra work because it's one of your own; we stayed out there all night. We found a couple of people who told us what actually happened. He had used cocaine and that induced a heart attack."

The gun was pointed at my partner. It was all a split-second thing," remembers Detective Richard Popp. "We ended up getting the gun out of his hand. I was able to get the gun away because I'm a lot bigger. Another guy tried to grab the gun out of my holster. There was a big fight on the street. We all went down. He pled guilty to attempted robbery."

"Jerry had the cuffs on him," Popp says, describing another incident. "The guy went crazy. The guy was swinging with cuffs over his head. I dove and grabbed his legs. We called for backup. I pulled Jerry's radio out of his back pocket. The crowd was screaming. They didn't start throwing things. They were just wound up. I told the crowd, 'Get the fuck back.' Everyone started backing up. You have to get as many cops as quickly as possible. One-oh-nine and Madison. He was five-nine, a solid two hundred and ten pounds. We were punching the guy's balls and upper body. He said, 'I just didn't want to go in, I didn't want to go to jail.' "

In 2000, New York City cops made over 400,000 arrests. Twenty-third Precinct officers arrested almost 1500 in the seven major crime categories: murder, rape, robbery, assault, burglary, grand larceny, and auto theft. The majority were for robbery. By contrast, the 19th Precinct had 3,958 arrests, the majority for grand larceny, which includes theft of personal property of $1,000 or more.

"The blue wall of silence," says Tara Casey, "does exist. It's the fear of being a rat, of giving up another cop. It's just silence. You don't take it upon yourself. If something very tragic or dramatic happens, you keep your mouth shut. You have the opportunity to say something anonymously during the investigation. People who can't stand each other will give each other up. It doesn't have to do with loyalty. You don't want to put up with harassment. If you give up someone, you ratted on somebody."

Years ago, it was considered the norm for police to receive Christmas gratuities, food and free services, such as dry cleaning, from neighborhood merchants. The cop who didn't was looked upon as an outsider and mistrusted.

Uniformed officers made drug arrests until 1972, when Detective Frank Serpico detailed corruption of high-ranking officials as the Knapp Commission uncovered payoffs to officers who overlooked gambling and drug trafficking.

Some cops are described as "sheep" by their colleagues, and if they don't associate with a group of solid, honest cops, they could be in trouble. "It's peer pressure," said one cop.

"One bad one influences the rest," says another. "Frank Serpico said ten percent were incorruptible, ten percent were looking for ways to steal, and eighty percent would adjust to the prevailing attitude. Stealing is a form of male bonding."

Police officers are forbidden to accept gratuities and free or discounted services or goods. A captain spoke of a PBA delegate in another precinct who still received free food and dry cleaning, even though he didn't work in that precinct anymore. A few cops in the Two-three knew where they could receive a discounted meal at a restaurant on 86th Street, in the 19th Precinct. Even the detectives who guarded the mayor ate there. Another knew where in the 23rd he could grab a free soda or two, or a Cuban sandwich. Some cops see nothing wrong with a free coffee; others, when their money is refused, leave it on the counter.

"Gratuities—I know that went on," says Sergeant Columbo. "My family comes from businesses. They'd demand whatever the fuck they want. My father had a bakery. He threw them [cops] out. They retaliated. They would summons our vehicle for deliveries. He went after that cop physically. The cop never walked that part of First Avenue again."

"I see nothing wrong with a discount or a free lunch," offers a captain who, in spite of his feelings, said he refused—or tried to refuse—a discount or a free lunch as a cop and as a ranking officer. "When we went into this deli in the Twentieth Precinct, the guy wouldn't charge us. I told him, 'If you don't take my money, I won't come here again. I can't shop in your place if you can't take my money.' I stopped shopping there. Another time I had no money. I hadn't eaten in a day and a half. I needed something to eat. On Amsterdam at Seventy-fifth Street, I knew I could get a pizza for nothing. All the police went there and took advantage. The police knew to go to certain restaurants in the Two-oh. They went in by seniority. Everyone knew where they were eating, so you didn't want to hit the guy twice. You rushed your food because they took good care of you. At another place the bill was a hundred and fifty dollars or something. They wouldn't take my money. 'You don't understand,' the waiter says. 'You don't pay here.' I left him ninety dollars for a tip and I never went back."

"**C**orruption is not organized, as it used to be," says a detective. "Twenty, thirty years ago, you were told 'Joe the Butcher. You get an envelope.' I think it's sporadic and probably in every busy precinct because they lowered the standards [to join the force]. With these cops, it's a crime of opportunity, just like a perp— because they lowered the [entrance] standards. Two collars with two armed robberies, applying for the Police Department? I don't care if the case was dismissed. Even in a case of mistaken identity, something happened. Then they ride around in a police car, chasing bad guys and getting into a shootout."

A cop says that to report corruption, "You're supposed to write a letter and put it in a sealed envelope, or come out and say it to a supervisor or call Internal Affairs." One officer says it should be reported to the precinct commanding officer. Another disagrees: "He doesn't want a corruption investigation in his precinct. Whose name gets dragged through the mud? And if he's in line for a promotion, he'll never get it."

"I would never give my name," says a cop. "I would never call. I wouldn't do it. It would have to be serious. Nothing with physical force or perjury. It has to do with corruption. I wouldn't want to get involved. Internal Affairs wants you to do more. They'll tell you to do fieldwork. That's their job. That's why I won't call. They'll do a six-month investigation. They'll find everything wrong except what I called them up for. For what? You'll hurt twelve ways and that dirtbag will still be running around. They're not going to leave empty-handed."

"I love my job. It's exciting," says Sergeant George Schulz. "You get everything in one ball of wax. You get to help people and you get to meet people. I love meeting people," says the forty-year-old sergeant with a brush cut. "I like being scared, to an extent. I've never had a complaint. If you go out and do what you have to do in good conscience, everything else doesn't matter. It doesn't stop you, it doesn't devastate you. It's not the end of your life. I'll allow myself to be pissed off, but I won't let it drag me down. I've been pretty lucky."

Schulz's father was a cop who had served in World War Two and retired in 1963. He spent eight years as a detective but was demoted back to a footcop in Brooklyn after "he refused to pick up the envelope," says Schulz. "That's the way the Police Department conducted business. He didn't want to have anything to do with corruption. Certain stores wanted extra protection. They threw money out to the precinct and the lieutenant would pick up the envelope and give everyone their cut. There were a lot of people who didn't want anything to do with it, including my father."

Dicks and Vics

*There is no hunting like the hunting of
armed men, and those that have
hunted armed men long enough and
liked it, never care for anything else
thereafter ...*

Detectives Jerry McGinnis and Bryan Lorenzo sign out in
the office logbook, underneath Ernest Hemingway's quotation
taped to the wall. They drive straight into gunfire on Second Avenue and 103rd Street. A black man with a nine-millimeter Sig
Sauer pistol has fired two shots. The two detectives heard only the
sound of the gunshots; they don't know how many men have guns
or who they are firing at. McGinnis calls in urgently over the police
radio, "Shots fired! Man with a gun!" and they jump out of their
unmarked car. McGinnis spots a pistol pointed at him and fires.
The man with the gun is down.

Cops monitoring their radios flood the scene, from the rookie protecting the abortion clinic a block away, to the rookie manning the stationhouse telephone now speeding past the projects without his bulletproof vest. News and gunshots travel with lightning speed. Young men are running from apartments, lobbies, and benches, teenage girls join them with smaller children, everyone clamoring for a look. The wounded man winces in pain. He is on the ground near a dark playground.

"I'll get you next time, motherfucker," a black man, standing over him, warns, before disappearing into the crowd.

An ambulance arrives for the inevitable trip to Metropolitan Hospital as cops quickly cordon off the area to sightseers. Traffic is detoured and the duty captain shows up to investigate, yelling something at a sergeant who yells for the crowd to stand back. McGinnis arrives at Metropolitan Hospital just after the man he shot; by police procedure, he will be examined for trauma.

Ballistics tests come back later. It is McGinnis's bullet in the man armed with a gun that's been traced to a cop in the 19th Precinct who had reported it stolen from his car in Coney Island.

"Today, you can't shoot at someone running," Lorenzo explains. "You have the duty captain hovering over you, [and] you have a two-day affair if you fight or shoot; you have to speak to the district attorney. Years ago, there was no Internal Affairs, no problem, no investigation. Today, if you take a shot at someone, it's a fifteen- to twenty-day report. Was it justified? It tells you how times have changed. It's all computerized. And," he adds, "everybody sues everybody for everything."

"You can't second guess," adds Detective Richard Popp. "You don't know how you'll react until you're there. There are so many things that could happen. I think the danger is definitely real. I feel safer working with someone who is confident and knows what they're doing. Active guys see a lot more things than other cops. Other people don't see things."

Jerry McGinnis and Popp are steady partners in the 23rd Precinct's RIP unit—Robbery-in-Progress. Both cops' wives assume that birthdays, anniversaries, and holidays will most likely be celebrated without their husbands.

McGinnis was once shot in the stomach; the only person in his unit to have ever been wounded. He explains: "There was a shooting at One Hundred Forty-fifth and Lenox and Seventh. There was a time in the City when the number of cabbies being killed was going sky high. We approached a cab occupied by four males. One had done a double homicide. All were on probation or parole. Bad group of guys. I approached the rear passenger side door. The guy opens up with one shot. I was shot in the stomach. My partner threw me to the ground. The car started to move. We kept up. I tried to shoot the guy. He flew out of the cab. I tackled him by myself and my partner subdued him, and we placed him under arrest."

The bullet went right under his undershirt. "It hit the top of my belt. It only went in about an inch. All the years of doing situps, I was very, very lucky. It was a twenty-two-caliber revolver. I was bleeding. My friend called a thirteen; everyone was apprehended. The bullet kind of worked its way out. I grabbed the fat on my stomach—a small roll (it saved me—that's why I carry extra). I had the bullet in my hand. Getting shot," he says angrily, "isn't part of my job description.

"He was given five to fifteen, five years for attempted murder on a police officer, plus he was out on a robbery case.

"I knew I was shot. It was one of those things. I wasn't fazed by it. What was I going to do? Lay down?"

Detectives McGinnis, Lorenzo, and Popp wear jeans, sneakers, boots, flannel shirts, and the occasional sportcoat and suits as they try and blend in as much as they can in East Harlem. They are required to wear jackets and ties, but since their RIP squad is considered the best in the borough of Manhattan, the rules are relaxed. This elite group is noted for its eagle-eyed cops, professional demeanor, success rate, experience, friendly rivalry, and weekly Lotto pools. Paperback Webster's dictionaries sit on every desk, one next to a "Lucky 13" candle. Every week, Detective Hector Otero collects a dollar from everyone including the sergeant, kisses the lottery tickets for luck, and hopes to win the jackpot. They haven't won a dime yet, but are "optimistic." A briefcase is perched on top of a garbage can, and typewriters are tilted on their backs on tables so they have more room to fill out handwritten reports.

The RIP team is comprised of a portly Hispanic detective nicknamed "El Gordo" (The Fat One), who has a wicked sense of humor; Jennie Rodriguez, a gay Puerto Rican female detective, who complains about the men and how they work; Jerry McGinnis, an Irish cop with five kids who does everything—including eating his dinner—quickly and thoroughly; Bryan Lorenzo, a young Hispanic cop about to be promoted to detective who is a whirlwind of ideas and energy; Hector Otero, a vain Puerto Rican detective always perfectly groomed. There is also a white detective with surfer-style blond hair, another who gets nervous speaking in a courtroom but who is the boss on the street, a Puerto Rican detective who hand-washes his shirts in Woolite, and an Italian detective who endures jokes about how cheap his sportcoats are.

Instead of family photos, Polaroid photos pasted on white paper, of perps wanted for robbery, form a collage on the wall. The ages of the young men are between fourteen and twenty. Detective Popp: "Blacks are robbing blacks and Hispanics. Hispanics are robbing Hispanics and blacks. Whites get robbed because they are here to pick up drugs, or they're delivery guys. White or Chinese make up one out of every twenty robbery complainants. Just because you're using drugs and you've been robbed doesn't mean it's not a robbery."

Cases are not as simple as they may seem. A man and a woman each claim that the other has stolen money. "No one will know—it's either him or her," Popp says of the couple. "Don't know who is telling the full truth. You don't know, you really don't know. How is anyone going to know? There are no absolutes in the world. There are so many robberies. The robbery unit, that's all we do. Years ago, the Police Department couldn't have been bothered."

The accused man had been incarcerated for robbery. "He violated parole in another state, where he did two armed robberies. They'll put him away for a long time. He was on probation until 2000. He moved to New York and transferred his parole to here. The girlfriend reported that he robbed her. He accused *her* of stealing four hundred and twenty-five dollars from his backpack, and a beeper. They were at her house. When he got to his house, he made a petty-larceny charge against her. He got a court order of protection against her. You can get a court order of protection against anything. He changed the stories and it mentally drained me. Everything is a technicality. There are cases piled in every room. One percent go to trial. It's sheer numbers, like a stockyard with cattle, dealing with cases. It's like running a marathon."

A black man sits in a chair, his hands shaking. He was robbed of his Social Security check in his building. His wife had to convince him to report it stolen.

"People are afraid," says Detective Popp. "You're in fear of someone being thrown from a roof. Things in this neighborhood are done for a number of reasons. A woman visiting a friend robbed her, took all her clothes. A neighbor wrapped her in a blanket. She never called the police."

Detective Pat Porteus has his coat on, hoping to leave early, but the pizza place around the corner is robbed twice that evening, the second time by eight kids. A Chinese delivery man is robbed for the fourth time this month. "Kentucky Fried Chicken would call me every three or four weeks that they were being held up," he says. "And in one store, apparently employees were stealing the money and covering it up by calling in robberies."

Crime fighting strategies now emphasize more thorough investigations. Someone arrested for possession of drugs is questioned about other crimes, in the event that they may have information to contribute.

Detective Popp says, "The basic philosophy hasn't changed—we still arrest people. The strategies have changed, but the philosophy hasn't. Now they want you to look for more perps and [we're] getting out of the office more. For me, I like to be out there.

"They want you to get out there, but if you're out there you'll run into something. They want two arrests a month. Some people are not making arrests.

"I'm great with the paperwork," he admits. "Paperwork takes three to four hours a day." Forty percent of the day he is in the office, fifty percent in the street.

After cops make an arrest, their suspect is photographed, fingerprinted, frisked, and the paperwork is completed, then he or she is taken down to Central Booking. The prisoner is placed in a cell and waits to be seen by a judge for arraignment. Unlike the movies, an alleged criminal in custody does not need a Miranda warning unless being interrogated.

Cops are judged by their arrest rate; assistant district attorneys by their rate of conviction.

"A cop could have the highest conviction rate and no one would know it. You're judged by your arrest rate," Popp confirms.

"If the DA is nice and professional, you go that extra yard. If the DA wants to play games and have an attitude, you can ask the DA not to put the case on. The DA can try and get it cancelled. Some DAs know that and some don't. Everything's a big game.

When you lock someone up and they beat it, fuck it. It's all a game. You'll get them the next time. We got to get him better the next time.

"The Assistant DAs have a won-lost average. They want a case that's indictable. You can't just dismiss it or that affects their batting average."

Homicide cases have expert ADAs; new ADAs start off with misdemeanors. Popp explains: "If you end up getting a young cop and a young ADA, they're going to learn through the school of hard knocks; they're going to fuck it up. People get screwed by their lack of experience. You learn not to embellish on anything. It gets you in trouble and you end up perjuring yourself. You just tell them what happened."

"DAs know the cops," he says. "The cops have a reputation. They know who's credible and who's sharp, and who isn't. Some are lazy, some are incompetent, some come to work. They'll cut deals because of cops.

"We have a stack of perps. The precinct is one square mile; there's a lot of warrants. A lot of it is for drugs. It takes some getting used to. With Jerry," Popp says of his partner, "we have very similar styles. It's hard to find two people who work together well. I'm very aggressive. Jerry works the same way. He always wants to get out [there]. We both see the same things out on the street. Everyone's got their own thing. There are [cops] who don't want to work. The other person can conduct the investigation. They want you to work at this level, and some people are up here and some are down here. Jerry and I are up here," he says, holding his hand above his head. "Some people only make a phone call. You can always do more. There's always something. You can canvas a building every day but it's not practical. You only have so much time. Do you want to go this far? Jerry and I, we're not going to cut back, even a little. Whether you bring in a collar at nine or at five, they bitch about the overtime."

Their files are filled with over two hundred names of suspects arrested in the last two years for robbery. Ten percent are women.

"Their entire life," Popp says of criminals, "is spent in the area where they live. A lot of guys reside on One Hundred Ninth, say. They get a little older, they have an apartment somewhere else, but come back and do their dirt on the block. And they more or less recruit kids from the block they used to live on."

"A lot of poor people are working people. They don't have the time to commit the crime. The younger element takes money for drugs, to go to the movies. The robberies, the muggings, it's a little different than a middle-class neighborhood. Most minorities are the biggest victims. We stop people in the neighborhood. In Chinatown, we're going to stop the Chinese. In white neighborhoods, we're going to stop whites."

A handwritten confession:

Tony came to my house, and told me to come with him to get something. We left the house and walk to 125th St and 2nd Ave to take the bus got off at 94th st walk to some project. he told me to wait down stair. Will he go up. 15 min later he came down and we went in the exit and gave me the belt it had buit [bullets] *on it. And I ask him how many buit the gun takes he said 7 shot. So we leff and walk down 2nd Ave 106th st so he told me the scape broke and the gun was sledin down. So we turn down to par Ave to go home when we got arrested.*

"I had this weird notion that I could make a difference," says Detective Willie Mendez, throwing up his hands. "That went promptly out the window. I've been able to find fulfilling things in this job. You see the battered wife who doesn't want to prosecute. You tell her her options and her rights. Latin women—for centuries—it's taboo to go to authorities. They can't believe that they have an out. The mother who calls the police and wants her son arrested. Stealing all the things in her house. Sometimes they talk to you like you're their son. Sometimes they want you to make the decision for them. In an odd way, you give them your opinion. Most of the time they'll make the decision. These are times that break my heart.

"My brother died in my arms," he says quietly. "He was murdered. He was twelve. He was my baby brother. It was a neighbor who did it. That was a long time ago. It made a big hole in my heart. I cried so many tears in my life that I have no more tears to shed. This guy was stalking my brother. He went to jail. He did maybe six years. The guy's father did time.

"I think a lot of crime goes unreported. I think in general people just count their losses and thank God they're still alive. Why go through the trouble? Pick up the pieces and start over. Most drug dealers won't report robberies unless shots are fired. We're here to help the people of the neighborhood. We investigate robberies. We're not the drug police. There are nice people out there if you take the time to talk to them. You still have to realize that there are decent people. I always try and leave off with, 'If there's anything I can do for you, give me a call.' "

Knowing how to talk to people—to schmooze them—is an integral part of solving cases. Cops are not merely arresting someone; they have to find him or her first, and speak to victims and witnesses, family, friends, and acquaintances. An abrasive manner gets you nowhere.

Detective Mendez: "You have to deal with people in a way they understand. The biggest part of it is common sense and a good line of shit to get out of something. When you respond to a dispute, you don't have to use your nightstick or anything. People like to be treated with respect whether they did something wrong or not. That person will always come back to help you out. If you get into a fight in that area, he'll call to help you out."

*   *   *

A black man walking north on First Avenue stops an undercover car driven by Detectives Jennie Rodriguez and Bryan Lorenzo. He says that he had stopped at Papaya King on 86th Street and Third Avenue and started walking home. Two black teenagers armed with a razor blade robbed him of two rings, three necklaces and an eighty-dollar watch. "Good thing I wasn't wearing my Movado," he adds, ignoring two cuts on his cheek. "It was a nice evening. I thought I'd walk home."

"Man, by my own people!" the victim says with disbelief. "I hate this city. I don't have any luck."

"What did they take?" Rodriguez asks.

"Two rings, three necklaces . . ." He pauses and begins to cry. "My dignity."

"It's been a long day for me. I've developed body odor already," notes Detective Billy Moore, sniffing at his underarms.

From 6:30 to 9:30 this morning, eleven people, including two doctors from Metropolitan Hospital, have been hit by pellets from a BB gun fired from a window in the Washington Houses projects. One BB is imbedded in a woman's head and has to be surgically removed. Another victim has been hit in the chest. Detective Moore narrows the trajectory down to the B line of apartments in one building; he and his colleagues go door to door, walking up and down stairs, knocking and ringing bells. They find their man in apartment 6B hiding under the bed, a teenager who thinks it's fun to shoot off a BB gun. Moore, a light-skinned black man with a thin mustache, rolls up his shirtsleeves as he begins typing up his paperwork, talking quietly to himself.

"This is like *Barney Miller*," Detective Jan Culley says with a laugh. "We have a guy who's always early, then we have the party animal. Every time I get stressed out I start cleaning, so they started calling me Detective Hazel. This is the cleanest precinct I've ever worked in," she adds. "But it's never going to look *that* clean." She looks over at Detective Eddie Martinez, a man in his fifties who refuses to wear glasses, so he reads complaint forms through a large magnifying glass. "Get glasses," she calls out good-naturedly. "You're well over forty!"

The daughter of two detectives—her mother was a policewoman who was offered a detective shield as a wedding present—Culley became a cop in 1982 after spending four years as a mental hygiene therapy aide. "I worked with an adolescent unit. You have to be really fuckin' crazy to be in a state hospital at twelve or thirteen," she says. "I quit in 1980—I was losing my mind. I went to work as a maid in a hotel for a year, and then I was promoted to desk clerk at the hotel. Got a job as a child care worker. I was the token white worker. Everyone else was black and they treated me like gold. As an aging hippie, by the time I left I was making twelve thousand dollars, and I also cleaned houses on the side. I took the police test. My parents believed that you take every city test, from garbage collecting to squirrel hunting.

"I went to a lot of DOAs [Dead On Arrival] as a rookie. People always treated you good. I worked in Crown Heights. Black men are used to stronger black women, so they weren't scared of strong white women. We would tell war stories in the car. I loved that shit."

Detectives sit at two rows of desks armed with telephones, separated by a low cement partition. The walls are covered with wanted posters. An interrogation room and holding cells are on the left, a coatrack is full of tan trench coats. Of the fifteen detectives, nine are Hispanic men, including Freddy Gonzalez, nicknamed "Burrito Boy" for his culinary interests and not-so-trim waistline. Two are African-American men; one Haitian; two women (one is raising two small children); Tommy Lombardo, bald and white, with more street savvy than most cops; and another, an older white man with a heart problem.

The two sergeants are a combination of old and new—Luther Barnes, a black veteran sergeant who worked as a cop during the race riots of the '60s, and Bobby Losada, a rookie Hispanic in his first assignment. The lieutenant, Anthony Lopez, still a handsome and trim man in his sixties, who only pretends to be gruff, is planning to retire.

Detectives work five days a week, and they work on four to five *dozen* cases at a time.

"We've spent hours trying to crack some of our homicide perps. You use every technique to get them to give it up," explains Detective Eddie Martinez. "Very seldom will you get a perp who says, 'Yeah, I did it.' It doesn't happen that way. Eighty percent won't admit to anything. You have to do a lot of legwork. The hardest part is trying to get a witness that someone did shoot someone. Their info may be hearsay, but it leads us in a direction.

"When children are involved in the drug trade, the mothers do expect that call," says Detective Martinez, putting down his magnifying glass. "When the parents are aware, ninety percent expect that they'll meet some type of violence. But a lot of parents deny that their kids are involved. They know, but they don't want to believe that it's happening. Ninety percent are drug-related homicides or felonies, felonious assaults. Where you have a crew working the streets, they're in business for themselves. They're territorial. They have disputes which turn into homicides, so that crew won't work the corner anymore. Only fifty percent of felonious assaults are by shooting. Disputes not involving guns are maybe twenty to thirty percent. Burglaries—the idea is to sell the property and buy drugs. Rapes—people that know each other, like a common-law wife. Robberies—you find that a lot are bogus."

"It's gotten worse," says Detective John Bartlett. "[There's] a lot of juvenile crime. With drugs, you don't have that many innocent victims. We've never been able to control the drugs. Drugs are involved ninety-five percent of the time, if not more. Who the hell wants to come forward? Robbery is more personal. With homicide, people ask, 'Why should I be a witness?' At One Hundred Tenth and Lexington, the projects are worse, drugwise. Every building has someone selling drugs. One Hundred Twelfth and Fifth, cars are triple-parked. Angel dust you can smell as soon as you walk in."

"Oh, fuck!" a young Hispanic man cries out, sitting in a chair in the office. "She didn't want me to be with her. I was with my daughter, man. She sent cops to my job. She's eighteen. Man, look, I don't want to call my father. I'm going to call my job. She said she was going to send the cops two days ago, but I didn't know. I went to work. The girl flipped out and said that I raped her.

"Right now, she's harassing my house," he wails and starts to cry. He is allowed to use the telephone to call home. "I got arrested for rape," he says, trying to keep his voice under control. "I didn't do it."

He hangs up the phone and speaks to Detective Bartlett.

"Somebody blew out all the lights in the stairwell," the young man says, standing next to a green metal desk covered with papers. "We always walked. She came into the stairwell on the fourteenth floor. We were talking in the stairwell. All of a sudden, the stairwell door opens. A big, black man, a Housing cop, came in. We ran. We knew he was going to say that we busted the light. I came back an hour later and there's a million cop cars," he recalls.

"A friend of mine said, 'They're looking for you. Something about a rape.' They jumped on me. The carted us off to the Eighty-fourth in cuffs. My mother fainted. The detectives came four hours later and they said the girl was lying. I was so glad. I found out later that her mother put her up to it because she lost her virginity. It was a cover-up so 'We can explain how you lost your virginity.' 'You know I didn't rape you,' I told her."

"Now, you're giving the guy a criminal number," explains Detective Bartlett about the alleged rapist. "There's a number that'll always be in the system. It is sealed, but you can get into it. Even if they purge the photo, there's still a photo lying around somewhere. You've planted a seed for a perfectly innocent fellow. It's not good if you're applying for a government job. There's a possibility of being turned down. You were arrested and fingerprints were taken. You have to have in mind [that] you're affecting their future. You have to be right. You just don't arrest someone with impunity. You have to have probable cause. Disorderly conduct is a violation. It's an arrest. It's an arrest, but the crime is a violation. No fingerprints are generated."

Elderly people are found dead of natural causes, others beaten, burned, and stabbed. "A guy was found dead on the roof," says Detective Bartlett. "It was his boyfriend [who did it]. And we had a guy shot with a nine-millimeter gun. There were no witnesses. But we came up with the girlfriend and came up with the gun. A guy ended up being locked up. It was a little dispute among themselves.

"Today, an ex-boyfriend made a menacing report against his former girlfriend. It's her word against his. You give him a desk appearance ticket because you don't know which way to go. You have to sort out the half truths. He hit her and she came back with a bat. Nineteen years old, she had a kid. She came into twenty-eight thousand dollars from an accident and it's all gone. He took the car. Did the girlfriend harass him? Yes. She's never been arrested. Why embarrass her? I'm not going to arrest her and I'm not going to arrest him. But I'm supposed to be doing something."

Another Hispanic teenaged girl recants her rape story and receives a desk appearance ticket, a misdemeanor, for filing a false report. "She was mad that he dumped her, so she made it up. The arrest was voided," says Detective Martinez. "After it was all done, she asked the non-rapist if he wanted to go out. She was flitting about the stationhouse. She asked if the fingerprinting process could be speeded up because she had to go to a party. A friend of hers was being sent to jail and they were throwing her a party."

Detective Bartlett: "We had a case down the block. The perp was in the apartment. Me and Billy Moore went out on the fire escape. We saw a hand put a gun on the fire escape. The hand was white. And there were four black guys. It was a junkie, the son of a stockbroker, and he stood out. Filthy fuckin' apartment, I had the heebie-jeebies for days," he says, shivering. "He took his mother's car and his father's car and traded them for drugs. He was arrested for falsifying a police report. He had filed a report saying that they were stolen. The family got both cars back. He took them for thousands of dollars. They lived in Scarsdale, a well-to-do neighborhood. His father gave him sixty-five thousand dollars. He devoured that in six months. They have the same problems as everyone else."

"One murder, one beating, a few domestic violence calls." He calls out the day's tallies to Detective Culley. "One Mexican shot two blacks, now they're trying to get even. It was the same gun. The Mexicans were found on a different street. One lived above the other with two kids under two piss-soaked diapers. You missed it."

"**M**other's Day is the busiest and so is the summer. The women are very submissive," says Detective Culley. "They have to satisfy everyone else. You're last. It's machismo to control your wife and everything in your household. You're the wife. You have the kids to think about. You have the guy who works. He beats you up. They think it'll be better the next time. I've seen mothers come in with sixteen-year-olds. One brought in the daughter who was pregnant by the boyfriend. He was abusing her and the mother-in-law. She was only sixteen. They get into elder abuse. Grandparents don't want to prosecute. It's very hard for the elderly to prosecute. Nobody likes to get beat up. Nobody likes a black eye. Nobody likes a bruised nose. There's some type of love. They're not beating them twenty-four hours a day. You have feelings for this person. Others are trained that it's acceptable. Human beings live on hope. There's always that hope. The homicides come after the woman leaves the relationship."

At Lexington and 113th Street, two friends were drunk. Detective Martinez says, "They dissed one of these four guys, who pulled out a gun and shot him in the head. We found everyone involved in dealing drugs. Eventually one of them cracked.

"With homicides you have to be a salesman. You're selling someone that's dead. You have to bullshit and tell witnesses what you can do for them. You have to tell them what they want to hear."

A man comes in and insists that his sister is missing. "Two guys told him that four guys picked her up, killed her, and dumped the body," says Detective Bartlett, taking down information and promising to investigate.

"My sister did drugs, four guys went looking for her on One Hundred Eighth and Lexington," the man says. "She went to sell drugs on One Hundred Ninth. Hadn't seen her in a while."

In another case, Detective Martinez passes around a Polaroid photograph of a bloated body in a bathtub, the eyes bulging and cartoonlike with a large, swollen tongue. "She died of a drug overdose in a crackhouse. The mother came up from Florida and they couldn't have her lying where she was. They put her in the bathroom and went about their business."

A drunk Mexican reported being robbed and his wife kidnapped. The Detective Squad has to treat it as an abduction and investigate. "We had to find out where the wife was. Did he kill her? It took four hours of investigation with seven people working," says Detective Bartlett. "The man had no wife. We arrested him for filing a false report."

Detective Martinez: "A fourteen-year-old girl lost her virginity to a fourteen-year-old classmate. She thought she was pregnant. She told her father, who was strict, and she said that this boy had raped her. After detectives questioned her, she admitted that she made it up. "I told him, 'You're going to lose her if you're so strict.' She'll be leaving at sixteen."

"What has affected me most is the death of little children," says Sergeant Barnes, removing his glasses and looking off into space. "My first homicide was a baby that died of alleged crib death at eight or nine months. They were two twin babies. When we arrived, both babies were dead. Same night, same crib. That really bothered us.

"Then there was a two- or three-year-old. The mother put the baby in the tub. The water was running. The baby touched the stopper and it fell in. The stopper closed, the water accumulated, and the baby drowned.

"A man killed six people, six homicides. I went to the funeral home to see six coffins lying in a row. We had the guy and we had to treat him as an individual. We fed him. It wasn't our place to judge him."

Sergeant Barnes was one of the first detectives at the scene of the Happy Land fire, an unlucky name for such a disaster. A man, angry with his girlfriend, set fire to an illegal social club in the Bronx, trapping eighty-seven people inside.

"Happy Land—that was unbelievable. I don't think that many people in the Police Department have experienced that. Someone said that there were eighty people killed. I said, 'Stop BS-ing me.' I was the first man in after the area was secured. The only space that you had to walk was in between the bodies. You had to step between arms and legs. Most died of smoke inhalation. Only two or three were actually burned. I couldn't believe it. I can close my eyes and still see the people lying there throughout the club. I coordinated and set up the removal of the bodies. The families were hysterical. We photographed each and every one of the victims for the families to identify. We put up a sheet so that family members wouldn't see the others. We opened up a school and laid out all of the photos and had the families look at the Polaroids. You can't disassociate yourself with that. I had a job to do. I had to manage myself. I saw all eighty-seven of them. I gained a reputation as Sergeant Death. It's a sight that will always be in my memories as long as I live."

Thomas L. Lombardo, Jr. used to be Shield 729 but, with the 1995 merge between the Police and Housing bureaus, has now become Shield 5371. Promoted to detective in 1987, he was raised in Harlem.

"My father took numbers in Harlem. Then he bought a car wash in Queens in the early 1960s. My mother was a burlesque dancer in the Latin Quarter. I think my father met her there. She died of cancer in September of 1973."

Lombardo repaired copy machines and drove a cab for a car service in the Bronx. "Then I took all city tests for pensions and benefits. I didn't know what a Housing cop was," he says. "They were the ones that called. Before I knew it, I had a month off at the time, twenty-seven vacation days. I loved the hours, the excitement, the time off. When you're single, the money is good. You don't have to answer to hardly anyone. I became active, I made a lot of arrests.

"The projects are their own little city. I got noticed. Others didn't want to work. I grew up in the Bronx. A lot of my friends were involved in gangs. When you get your first couple of homicides, it's surprising. You've got to be mentally ready. You develop

alligator skin. You don't want to break down. You joke around
and you put it behind you. Not even a dead baby, nothing affects
me. Nobody likes to smell a DOA. The smell stays with you. You
become immune to this type of thing," he says.

Detective Lieutenant Anthony Lopez directs his squad from a
corner office, old enough to be the father or grandfather of most
rookie cops. The New York City Police Department's mandatory
retirement is sixty-three. "For every day I spend out here, one less
day at home," he muses. "I'll be sixty-three. Why stay any longer?
I went to the end. I think I stayed too long—there's been a lot of
changes. It seems to me, crime is down. It's the whole aspect of
attacking crime and upgrading the Department. The job is revert-
ing to where a cop is a cop, not just a report taker. It's not going
to change overnight. The complaints never really change. The Department has to serve the people. We give them what they're entitled [to]. You're always pitted against the guy you're locking up.
Very few people go easy. There were always rumors that cops do
this and cops do that. How true they were? Probably as true as
the fact that we throw people off the roof. Does life follow the
movie or does the movie follow life?

"Reporting rape was a radical change before the law was
changed. I think that more cases are reported. There's less of a
stigma with rape. Years ago people had cancer and it was whis-
pered. Now you have a more enlightened, more informed society.

"There was a movie with Pat O'Brien and George Murphy. They
would sit around in uniform all day at Fifth Avenue and Park
Avenue. They would go to a secret entrance and have tea and
coffee with the maids. Today, you have a totally different portrayal.

"I don't know what people would expect of a cop of today." He
pauses. "I'm at a different stage in life. I don't expect anyone to
be James Bond like some kid coming on the job thinking he's
going to be shooting down everybody."

He was saddened by the fact that one murder hadn't been

solved. "Paola Illera, in 1991, was a young girl found stabbed on the FDR Drive. Someone found her as they were walking by the One Hundred Second Street Bridge; she was fully clothed. We never knew how she got there. She rang the bell to her building on One Hundred Eleventh Street. She never came up the stairs. It was three-thirty to four p.m. She just came from school. She was found at five-thirty to six p.m. Never knew how she got there. No indication of who had done it. The family was Colombian— very good people. They buzzed her in, she never made it upstairs. The family was living with other relatives. It was a young girl. There was no reason. No apparent reason for her killing," he says quietly. "They were devastated. They call from time to time. Not much you can tell people."

The girl's killer would be arrested and convicted a decade later.

Down and Dirty

"I started dealing crack," says thirty-one-year-old Martin Velez, who lives on 115th Street. "I got busted for heroin one time. I did four years. I never harmed nobody. Wheeling and dealing, I made seventy-five dollars a day, but I just got tired of it. That was a hard-earned seventy-five dollars. I was watching people hustle. I was watching people and the police. I was the lookout. I had no other choice. The other choices were robbing someone or snatching someone's chains. I don't have the heart for that."

"Jamaicans deal marijuana," says Sergeant Steve Ringe. "The Dominicans and Colombians sell coke at one hundred dollars a gram or ten to twenty dollars a blow. Crack and heroin—ten dollars for a three-gram bag—belongs to the Colombians.

"I think the heroin comes from Asia. Here, it's just the opportunity. The blacks tend to be chosen a lot as dealers. They live fast, make a buck, die young. Kids make fifty bucks in two hours. Here, it's a cultural thing how people spend their money. Just because people drive fancy cars doesn't mean that they're drug dealers. You go to some apartments—you find secondhand, broken, odd pieces. These people don't spend much on decorating, but women will own an eighty-dollar jumpsuit. There's nothing in the house. They spend all the money on the car or the clothing."

On One Hundred Twelfth, between Lexington and Third, a nineteen-year-old guy puts drugs in the mailbox of the housing project.

"An older guy and kids sell it," explains Officer Dave Argentina. "They pick up a brown paper bag and hide it underneath cars or car bumpers or in garbage cans. One man was using fourteen- or fifteen-year-old kids that we couldn't lock up for sale. He'd get kids lower and lower in age. There was a lot of police presence so they moved the drugs inside. Then the drugs were not as available for customers. You don't want to go into an apartment to buy drugs.

"These drug dealers are streetwise. They know when we work. They have tour changes just like we have tour changes. They've adapted to what we've done. Then we have to make adjustments."

Five cops man the 23rd Precinct's van with the broken door— the Street Narcotics Enforcement Unit. It has no air conditioning and the steering wheel cover is missing. Two cops in plainclothes and bulletproof vests, and carrying radios and binoculars, exit the van and enter a building. They will snoop on drug locations from a rooftop, looking for drug consumers. Some days it is slow, other days business booms.

"Drug dealers don't care about their effect on people," says Officer Argentina, who has been an undercover cop for almost six years. "Six pounds of coke could be made into thirty-six thousand vials of crack worth about two hundred thousand dollars. You really don't deal with anyone over thirty with drugs. They start at sixteen and they either get killed or go to jail by the time they reach their twenties. They conduct business like they're sales people. A vial of crack, a welfare check—it's party time."

On television, street-level drug dealers drive flashy cars and wear fancy clothes and jewelry. In East Harlem, they don't leave the neighborhood. Their working conditions are so terrible that, if theirs was an honest job, they'd form a union. They stand on corners and in doorways until the early hours of the morning—steerers and dealers—in the rain and cold, in the snow.

An economics professor analyzed data that detailed the financial activities of a drug gang over a four-year period. Like a corporation, a small group oversees them and turns a large profit, but almost one-third are in prison at any given time. Gang leaders, the report says, earn about sixty-five-dollars an hour. Street-level drug dealers average just three dollars an hour, hoping for a promotion. The odds of suffering the occupational hazard of being killed are one in four. The dealers feel that cops have no business in their savage life, no right to interfere.

"I know a lot of drug dealers out here and I respect them as human beings," says James de la Cruz, a neighborhood resident. "We're all connected. I've had family members who are drug dealers. One was killed. Drug dealers, they're just like everyone else."

Perhaps they are most like police in their psychology. Rats—snitches—are detested, the brotherhood of the job demands that you stick by each other no matter what, and both are suspicious and assume someone is always up to no good. Officer Argentina estimates that half of the buyers are New York City residents, the rest come from out of state. The youngest seller he's caught was a twelve-year-old boy; the oldest, a seventy-two-year-old man. The SNEU (Street Narcotics Enforcement Unit) team averages three to six arrests a day in the spring and fall, four to eight during the summer, and during the colder winter months, two to four.

"There's potential for danger in this precinct," says Officer Argentina. "It's not going to happen on a regular basis. The danger is cops getting shot or attacked. That's my perception. There's a lot of decent people, a lot of drugs. A lot of the dealing is from behind closed doors. See the fancy cars and people. We know who they buy from, too. Drugs are packaged here or just being moved from Brooklyn and Manhattan to upper Manhattan. When there's drugs and guns, there's danger."

The police radio crackles. The rooftop team describes a black man in a red-and-blue striped shirt and blue jeans who has just purchased drugs. The van turns the corner and three cops jump out. The startled man stuffs vials into his mouth.

"Spit it out!" one cop orders. The man obliges, spitting three crack vials with purple tops into his hand.

The van begins to fill up. This sweep lands a black Con Ed worker, a white stockbroker in an expensive suit and tie who begins crying, a schoolteacher with a black bag, a hospital worker, and a hyperactive Hispanic woman with a ponytail arrested with forty-one bags of marijuana. "But no one really cares unless you're the CEO of a major company," Argentina explains.

"Do you think I'm a person with a problem, or just a piece of crap?" one of the men asks as this group is driven, handcuffed, back to the precinct.

"A person with a problem," Argentina answers quietly.

"Thank you for treating me like a person," says the man.

One curious cop turns around. "I don't want to hear anything about the case, but I'd like to know what it feels like to shoot up. I've been told that it feels like a thousand orgasms," he says.

"I don't feel anything," the junkie replies, leaning back against the seat. "I just take it so I don't get sick."

A black man observes it all from a street corner, while smoking a blunt and drinking a forty-ounce bottle of beer. He says he earns close to a thousand dollars a week selling crack. "Cops. I don't like them," he says, shaking his head. "I can't see myself being a cop. They got crooked cops and they got old cops. They ain't worried about drugs and money. Crooked cops I haven't seen, but I heard. I get followed. Mostly everybody gets followed. Sometimes some of them have binoculars and cameras on the roof. No, I never been called names. It's other people I got to worry about. There ain't no safe projects. Every time I walk out there I wonder if I'm gonna get shot or stabbed or killed.

"In terms of survival, it's survival of the fittest. It's dog eat dog. Police? I don't mess with those guys. You don't have to have nothing in your pocket. They're bugged out. They'll come and harm you if you don't have nothing. People understand more when you talk to them. 'Yo, get off the corner.' I ain't no dog, no animal. They need a school of respect. If I live in this building and I stand on this corner, I'm paying rent. That part of the sidewalk is yours. They don't look at it like that. I avoid all contact. I go the other way."

A twenty-two-year-old, who had served four years in prison for manslaughter, says, "What was I supposed to do? This guy was checking me out, checking my movements, if I didn't get him, he was going to get me. The rules are different out here. I know I'm not gonna live long. I was not put on this earth to live long. You cops are up all night, checking out my every move even when I'm taking a shit. I ain't doing nothing wrong."

Luis Roberto Cepeda—nicknamed "Papo"—was born in 1949, the oldest of twenty. His mother aborted seven. Of the thirteen,

one brother hanged himself at twenty-four, a sister contracted lu-
pus, swallowed rat poison, and died. Three of the eleven living
children have a high-school degree. Only one of the family is
working. All of the family worked in the drug trade. In the seventies Papo went to jail.

"I went to Danbury Correctional Facility. There I met a lot of
big dealers. I started doing bigger business in East Harlem. I
started doing big business in the house. It was crazy. I was always
hiding. People hardly saw me. I was running everywhere. In 1986,
I started smoking crack. In 1987, I went to Puerto Rico. I started
dealing over there. I made money you cannot believe. One million
dollars in eight months. Fourteen to fifteen thousand dollars a day.

"My brothers and sisters looked up to me. I was doing drugs.

"My brother, Juanito, served twelve years in prison. They
charged him with throwing a guy off a roof. I was smoking crack
more and more. I used to take an ounce and cook it. I would
smoke and smoke and smoke for five days."

He moved back to New York City where his family was. "I tried
to tell them, don't do this, don't do that. They learned on their
own. I didn't give them drugs. They saw it all the time. Ten-dollar
bags of cocaine in and out of the apartment. White people, black,
they used to come. When you got good stuff, they used to come.
We used to go someplace like Washington Heights or I used to
get a delivery for me. Heroin never caught my attention. I'm afraid
of needles."

Cepeda earned a high-school diploma, and he attended John
Jay College for Criminal Justice for two semesters.

"I wanted to be a policeman. I was living with my sister on One
Hundred Fifteenth Street. I had two kids at the time. Then my
brother started selling drugs, all the family was selling drugs. I
used to bring stuff to Mommy and she would sell coke, heroin.
Everyone got involved. We all started to go to jail."

Junkies, sharing needles supplied by his mother, shot up in the living room of their public housing apartment. He joined the Army in 1973, serving in Germany for two years before working for a Veterans Administration hospital as a filing clerk.

"I stayed for fourteen months. I was still doing coke. Then I started driving a flower truck. I was smoking, getting high."

Cepeda rejoined the Army and was sent to Germany and Fort Knox, Kentucky. "Then I went to school for a lab technician. I was getting high. We sold coke to the DEA. I did one year, one day, and then six months in a halfway house. One day, in the handball court, I was smoking a joint. My son comes up to me and says, 'Papi, I want to be like you.' I said, 'What? You want to be a junkie?' "

on cops' records and can be used against them if they're interested in moving into a specialized unit.

A complaint form is expected to be available on demand at precincts.

"Get the fuck out of here!" orders one sergeant at the 23rd Precinct.

"We don't have any available," says the cop in the complaint room.

"Why? You making a complaint?" asks another.

It costs thirty dollars to become a New York City police officer.

If a man or a woman is at least twenty-one, but no more than thirty-five-years-old, with two years of college and no felony convictions, a Civil Service test will initially decide whether they're police material or not. More a measure of reading comprehension than anything else, the four-hour exam is taken by a cross-section of New Yorkers from the city and suburbs every year. Some enter from the New York City public school system, others from Catholic and private schools, community colleges, Ivy League schools, and law schools. The Police Department attracts men and women who, in their previous lives have delivered mail, sliced sandwiches in a deli, driven a bus to Atlantic City, acted in off-Broadway plays, fancied themselves writers, managed a sales counter in a department store, trained in the military, walked through aisles of shops as security guards, drafted architectural plans, sold cosmetics, delivered newspapers, counseled others, typed invoices, illustrated magazines, traded stock on Wall Street, and repaired boilers and air conditioners. Some always dreamed of becoming cops or detectives, patterning themselves after a father, mother, or uncle in the business of policing. Others were inspired by Kirk Douglas in the movie, *Police Story*, or television shows like *Dragnet, The Rookies, Hill Street Blues, NYPD Blue, Law and Order*, and *Charlie's Angels*. Some desired the job security, pension, and benefits.

And still others have no idea how and why they ended up in the Police Department.

"It just gets in your pores," says a cop. "You can't imagine what it's like to be in a uniform and then you can't picture yourself out of it."

"In most businesses, you have more of a homogenous population," says Detective Jan Culley. "You don't have a homogenous population here. People are cops for a hundred zillion reasons. Sometimes you have nothing in common; sometimes you will have a lot in common. With the district attorneys, chances are they're fighting for truth and justice and they have the same law school experience. Here, you have people from PhD's to GED's and they might be partners."

It doesn't matter how they got there or why. After passing the Civil Service test they enter the Police Academy for six months, and learn to "serve and protect." These future cops undergo physical and psychological testing and training, classes ranging from legal rights to handcuffing and frisking a suspect, to driving a patrol car, down to how to knock at a door. They learn why, when, and how to use their guns, how to observe people, and they take classes in cardiopulmonary resuscitation, emergency treatment, and childbirth. Each potential police officer learns how a situation can change in a split second and how important it is to save their own lives.

But psychological tests do not indicate or cannot predict the limits of their patience, their reactions to seeing life and death situations in an eight-hour shift, their responses to hearing the same complaints day after day, to walking through garbage-strewn streets and elevators saturated with urine and roaches, or dealing with the politics inside of a precinct and within the Police Department. A number of people fail the psychological test. Some appeal and make it, others don't.

"I failed the psychological test," admits Sergeant Lawrence Av-

ery of East Harlem's Housing Police. He holds a bachelor's degree
from the School of Visual Arts. "You had to draw a self-portrait.
I did a very detailed drawing of me in a T-shirt with a stick figure
in the pocket. I was waving hello. The psychiatrist said, 'I don't
want you to draw a stick figure. Obviously, you can't follow orders.
You wouldn't be a good police officer.' I had to see my own psychiatrist for four sessions. That's part of the weeding-out process.
And then you had to draw a house and a tree. That cost me at
least a year. My tree had dream clouds and everyone was in it.
At the time, I was ambitious to be more than I was. I was earning
three dollars an hour. I drew a picture of my present home, a
colonial two-story with a two-car garage. The American dream
home, a good, middle-class home. The psychiatrist didn't like that,
either."

Affirmative Action and lawsuits during the sixties and seventies
added more women and minorities to the Department and elimi-
nated height and weight requirements. Back in the old days if a
cop stood half an inch less than five-ten, or had an outstanding
parking ticket, he was disqualified. Now, people sue when they
fail. Overweight candidates, who couldn't scale a wall and failed
the physical exam, claim that they have been discriminated
against. (Ironically, at a time when the Police Department was
actively promoting fitness, one cop in the Twenty Third—a PBA
delegate—was so obese that cops complained he broke the seat
supports in their patrol cars.)

Candidates over the age limit sued, claiming they, too, were
discriminated against. One veteran cop recalled the story of a
recruit failing the eye exam, but someone pulled strings, and the
candidate miraculously regained 20/20 vision. Another cop, a
chunky Hispanic woman with asthma so bad she would collapse
during gym classes, was painstakingly tutored through the Police
Academy after failing the written exam four times. A second His-

panic cop explained that her colleague only passed because of the
shortage of Spanish-speaking cops. The woman had even failed
the driving part of the training, which meant she could not drive
a patrol car.

Felony arrests pled down to misdemeanors enable still others
to qualify. "You're standing next to a rapist, a drug dealer, a
robber. How are you supposed to know this?" complains one cop.
A few possess such heavy accents they can barely be understood,
while some haven't the simplest writing skills needed.

After blacks and Hispanics complained and sued that police
exams were biased, Police Commissioner Ben Ward, who served
from 1984 through 1989, promoted minorities throughout the Department. He lowered the test scores on promotional exams and
created a B list. These minorities were quickly dubbed "quota
sergeants."

"You're fooling the public," laments one cop. "They think
they've got someone who knows how to handle themselves and they
don't. These cops could lose their lives. With Affirmative Action,
the job promoted people. It gave people titles who weren't qualified.
You've got people who can't do this job. They're not weeded out.
They push to get black males or females or Hispanics. From day one
they're telling them, 'Don't worry, I'll do it for you.' There's a scar
on this job that will be here for a long time. Until people say,
'Why do we have to hire fuckin' incompetent people?' A lot of
people on this job shouldn't be on this job. People say, How dare
you talk to me like that?' The only people who use racism are
people being called on the carpet. Fuckin' carpet to hide behind.
I don't see it changing. No one will say what they think."

After passing tests for psychological acuity and six months of
training, a harsh reality sets in. One cop recalls a day spent delivering a baby and then rescuing two children from a burning
apartment. Taking a breath and leaning against his patrol car for

air, he said he was greeted by an officer from the Inspections Unit, demanding to know why he wasn't wearing his hat. Cops can receive complaints for chewing gum, carrying or reading a newspaper, napping, taking too long on a job, or not answering the job at all.

"I think the Police Department feels that it starts by not wearing your hat—then the corruption starts. It's all bullshit," says another cop.

Internal Affairs investigates corruption by cops and also sets up stings, to see how honest they are. Cops tell stories of money or drugs left in apartments as bait, and drugs placed on windshields of patrol cars.

"They're starting this again?" complains one cop after she finds a paper bag filled with crack vials left on her patrol car's windshield. "Now we have to go back into the stationhouse and voucher this."

"In the Three-oh," recalls Captain Matt Carmody, "it was an 'us against them' mentality. They [corrupt cops] were drawn toward each other. They had that siege mentality. Whereas here [in the Twenty-third Precinct], there isn't a cohesiveness. There are enough separate groups here. They're not impressionable. People coming on the job are not as impressionable.

"This department won't use the word *quota*," he says. "It's *court mandated*. I would hate to be a black man or a black woman and be legitimately promoted. You would automatically be characterized as a 'quota sergeant.' You would not be given the same credibility. It's relative to the population you're serving. Even application investigation is a crock because it is so lenient. They're pushing the minorities—everybody who's not qualified. Affirmative Action? They're not looking for qualified people. They're looking for bodies."

*   *   *

"The whole idea of this job is to get off of patrol," says PBA delegate Alan Patrick. "There's sort of a caste system on this job. Right above patrol is CPOP (Community Policing), which is like living in the projects. SNEU (Street Narcotics Enforcement Unit) is a little better. Anti-Crime is the elite of the patrol force. Then you have RIP (Robbery-in-Progress) and the Detective Bureau. If this job was equated to life, the patrol would be the homeless. They're the lowest of the low."

Sergeant Aaron Barr taps a small Queen of Peace medal that he wears around his neck and watches the team from Emergency Services pack up their equipment. "Patrol—everything comes down to patrol. I believe that patrol is the backbone of the Department. You treat them well and you get more out of them. I've been there. I'm not going to treat them badly.

"Everybody's different. I thought everybody handled it the way that I did. The Police Department takes anybody that barely passes high school. Guys who basically passed the test go into the Police Academy and they push them along. Then they go to a precinct and on patrol. They shouldn't be on patrol in the first place. It's too dangerous.

"They should start letting go of people. People are confused, they can't make out reports. It's really bad, it's amazing how these people passed high school. A guy in my old command, who I locked up six months before, asked me to write a letter saying why he should be allowed on the job. I threw it in the garbage. He was a felon: Assault Two.

"Sometimes I feel like a big babysitter. I know females and males who shouldn't be on the job. That's tough. They're your responsibility no matter what they do. If you're not working the day that something happens, you sometimes have to hang for it. I used to like going to work." He groans. "I was afraid to take off, that I was going to miss something."

His brother, also a cop, worked with an officer named Ray

Cannon who was shot and killed by two men attempting to rob a store in Brooklyn. "My brother cried like a baby. He saw him die there. He was there within minutes. Ray Cannon's face was blown off. My brother was devastated," he says quietly, looking away. "It's all very arbitrary." He shrugs his shoulders. "These are the guys you need, guys like Ray Cannon. I hope the Department hasn't forgotten him. He did give great service to the city."

Sergeant Barr lets out a deep sigh. "Life goes on. In a few months, they'll forget about what happened, forget about Ray Cannon. Someone fills your spot in twenty-four hours."

"They get on jobs, they're scared," says a veteran sergeant. "They don't use their heads to control themselves. After five years, you mellow out. Rookies don't know what to do. They're told that they're in control, but they're not using their brain. Look at other places around the country. Cops are on patrol at forty. Everybody's looking to get out of patrol here."

Transfers off of patrol into special details, such as Anti-Crime, Emergency Services, and narcotics, are often made on the basis of a hook. The hook could be a friend or relative in the Police Department, or a connection who can pull strings. What cops say is, if the Police Department is looking to fill the spot with a female or a person who speaks a second language, that person might be placed into the position regardless of qualifications.

"There's a lot of bureaucratic bullshit," says one dissatisfied cop. "If you have a hook, you'll go somewhere. If not, you're fucked. It'll take you a bit longer. You don't get things on the basis of merit. Everyone's looking out for themselves. It's ridiculous what goes on."

"It's 'the Peter Principle,' " explains one captain, ruefully. "You promote to a level of incompetency. If you're an excellent patrol officer, then you're promoted to CPOP and SNEU."

"Most of the people who are here are incompetent fucks. I'm

responsible for all these people," one sergeant groans, echoing the captain's resentment. "With some people you just throw your hands up. You have to give them a little breathing room. They have to be supervised, watched over, directed. I have no other alternative. I really have to deal with them. Sometimes you hold your breath and hope that things turn out for the best. On the street, I'm more afraid of being shot by another cop than by someone else."

"They have no people skills," a cop complains of his supervisors. "Just because they pass a test doesn't mean they know how to manage people. The captain yells at lieutenants, who yell at sergeants, who yell at cops. They're yelling at us for a hundred and fifty years worth of incompetence."

Like CEOs of major corporations, most commanding officers are far removed from the day-to-day details and reality of fighting crime. Instead, they deal with paperwork, logistics, political pressures both from the Police Department and the community, and statistics. Commanding officers (COs) with ranks of captain, deputy inspector, or inspector, are moved around via promotion or transfer every two years. Every CO brings his own style, personality, tactics, and reputation into the precinct where he works. Heads of precincts are appointed by the police commissioner; cops and their union have no input. But like a difference between the upper class and working class, commanding officers are generally better educated and more ambitious. One cop suggests that they undergo psychological testing.

The rank and file complain about bosses:

"There's nothing rational about the captain. He's very bright but he doesn't know how to apply it. Decisions—you have no choice. You've got to do it."

"Petty. I think he's very petty. If you're not part of the club, then you're not going to make DI [deputy inspector]. The captain, he's not one of the guys. He buffaloes people, he bullies people. He treats them like shit. He beats up the cops and caters to the fuckin' perps. He's a horrendous boss. You have a CO who doesn't know much about patrol, doesn't care, and doesn't have a clue. He's one inexcusable, fucking bastard. He's not really well liked."

"He's a great bunch of people," a cop says, sarcastically. "He micromanages everything."

"Very, very bad personality. Don't know what to expect from him. Very short temper. God forbid you have a problem. He's the last person to speak to. You do something for him and he turns around and fucks you. He always comes up and says the numbers are down. No one does it for him. No reward benefits for being on patrol. Guys are idiots. You have to treat them like idiots. You have to push, then wind them up."

Not everyone agrees. Some like the boss:

"He should have been a great boss but they didn't promote him. It's not right what they did to him."

"I've seen the captain once in six months. The ones who complain about the captain are the ones who aren't doing anything. Who are they going to blame when they don't answer a job? It's their fault."

At the 23rd Precinct, one cop was called "stupid" in front of his colleagues by a captain. Stung by his words, the cop burst into tears.

A second cop, with a comprehensible and charming West-Indian accent, approached the desk sergeant, who ordered him to "speak English." The weeping cop had to be consoled in the locker room by several of his colleagues.

"If civilian complaints were given out to people here," another cop says, sardonically, "there would be more inside the Police Department than out on the street."

One veteran recalls his request for the day off on the anniversary of his mother's death. The captain refused, on the grounds that he should have recovered from her death by then.

Another sergeant blames the captain's personality. "We stay later for him," he argues. "He's always working on stats and he never says thank you. And when it comes time for dinner, he never says, 'Here, buy something for yourself.' If he treated people better, he'd get more work out of them."

An anonymous letter, slipped under doors, accuses bosses of destroying the morale of cops by denying requested days off and by changing their hours, putting them on rotating schedules—a week of days, then a week of nights, followed by a week of midnights, and then starting all over again. Cops hate this because it leads to erratic sleep schedules, interferes with second jobs, babysitters, and wreaks havoc with their personal and social lives.

New York City police officers are represented and protected by their own union, the Patrolmen's Benevolent Association. Sergeants, lieutenants, and captains have separate unions. Every cop is expected to be a dues-paying member of the PBA and each precinct has at least one, if not two or three cops elected as PBA delegates. The 23rd has three. Cops act as precinct "lawyers." If a cop has received a reprimand from the precinct commander or is charged with official misconduct, he (or she) contacts his PBA delegate, who may get the charges reduced or negotiate a deal. In more serious cases, the PBA has its own law firm which represents cops in legal matters involving police issues up to the time they are arraigned. Cops must then hire their own lawyers. A large voting bloc of members comprised mainly of Republicans, the PBA has its own lobbyists in Albany.

Police officers have a weapon against the mayor, the Police Department, and their commanding officer: summonses. Much easier to tally and document than arrests, summonses generate income for New York City. Rather than writing additional summonses for every infraction—which would create more work for them, and which would aggravate citizens, merchants, business people, and corporations into protesting to the Mayor's Office—cops write few or none. "If there was a problem, we could have a job slowdown where we don't write summonses. We'll stop writing summonses," says one PBA delegate. "It's the equivalent of a job action."

With all of their complaints about society losing respect for authority and, in turn, for police, cops are united against authority in the Department. Some cops rebel by not following orders; sergeants fraternize with the ranks below. A few assume an unprofessional appearance.

"People don't give a shit how they look," says Walter James a cop whose uniform and figure is trim and immaculate. "It's disgusting. They have no pride. You get a thousand dollars for a uniform allowance to keep up your uniform. That's what it's for. Look the part. You got the money. That's bullshit. I must have at least ten shirts, brand new pants. These guys wear the same pants for ten years. If they don't fit, they buckle them down here and the hem keeps getting higher and higher. We used to have inspection every day."

"The attitude towards authority is bad," says a sergeant. "The bosses here don't know how to demand respect. They try to be everybody's buddy. The cops call supervisors by their first name. Bosses get called to way too many jobs. You never want to call the sergeant; it shows you can't handle the job by yourself. People don't know how to fill out a dog bite report. There are people who can't enunciate, 'You're under arrest.' They leave it all to me. The job changed because it tolerates a lot more than what it used to.

They accept a lesser degree of competence. The job brought in more and more people, but now [they] have a gap in supervisors. A sergeant works with no direction from above. Cops used to find a boss that they could work with. It's the job's fault. Everybody passed, you're all on the list."

Morale is low, in a police department which sees itself working like a corporation. While a corporation offers raises, rewards, and incentives, the Police Department, citing Civil Service union contracts, cannot.

"What can they offer?" asks one cop. "And when you retire, all you do is throw your shield in a box. No thank yous. No, 'Goodbye, thank you for serving the people of the City of New York.' "

"Me and Mike had a robbery pattern," says Detective Willie Mendez. "Three perps robbing Mexicans. We caught the three perps and closed out the cases. Then Lieutenant Lopez says, 'What do you want? A medal? That's your job.' The satisfaction is more. What about the thousands of other heroes? We do this all the time. I'm very shy of cameras," he admitted. "I'm not looking for no glory. [But] the Department treats us as numbers. Why should you be looking for glory? You have a roomful of medals. But you mess up once and you're out of a job. It's scary. You have to try and be as thorough as you can so no one can find a fault, so no one can make you miserable. People get jammed up and they are not the do-nothings. If you do nothing there's no need for you to get jammed up."

A cop describes himself as a cynic: "I think I've always been this way. I'm a pessimist by nature. You have to write up citations yourself. My first medal, me and my partner rescued a woman with a two-year-old and a three-year-old from a burning building. The sergeant from the precinct told me and my partner that the battalion chief said if it wasn't for us they would have died. 'Make sure you write it up,' he said. It shouldn't be that way, writing up your own commendation. It's always nice when a higher-ranking boss pats you on the back and says, 'Nice job.' That's what kept me going in the Bronx. The inspector used to come around and he made you feel like you were the best cop in the world. He got a lot of production out of his people. He'd say, 'You guys are the best.' "

"What does someone have to do to get sympathy around here?" asks Anita Perez. "Die?"

Cops retaliate by doing less work, by writing fewer summonses. "Nothing gets done, they take their time getting to jobs," one cop mutters. "They don't write summonses. Guys turn out, buy all their papers and a coffee, and go to a corner and sit there."

Officer Paul Lawson recalls being an idealistic rookie: "About year five you stop caring. About year ten you start doing a countdown to your pension. I'm on year nine going on ten and I started my countdown already."

"The burnout goes in cycles," explains a sergeant. "Three years is the first time you feel like quitting. At six years, you're happy to be here and you change. The job itself has a lot to do with it. A cop should be able to make a decision. I came on at twenty-eight. I had two children. I'm not a person who likes to fight or to do anything in excess. I'll always go with the flow. I'm very mellow. The I.Q. of most cops is close to one digit. They're a bunch of jerks. The pay is good; it's not half bad. Then I found out you can still be an idiot and be a sergeant."

Alan Patrick's function as PBA delegate is to protect the men and women of his command.

"A lot of guys get fucked around for different reasons. Everytime something happens, it's patrol they go after. They don't go after people at headquarters; they go after the poor patrol guys. They're easy to find, easy to keep track of, and they're doing their jobs. You take too long to get to a job and they harass you. A strong delegate has to be someone who is an advocate. I think up stories for cops all the time. They know why they did it but can't articulate it. I'm like a lawyer for the cops. I'm there for shootings, get families to the scene if cops get hurt, illness . . . I love helping cops. I love making a couple of phone calls to help cops. It's a good feeling.

"A lot of people don't think cops are human. Cops are not afforded the same rights as citizens. Some of the guys are better than others. You're getting people from all different backgrounds. Not everyone is going to be the cream of the crop. Some young guys are on the job thinking they're the Law. I greet every class that comes in. I say to them, 'You're second-class citizens. Handle yourself as professional as possible. Don't think that drug-dealer piece-of-shit on the corner isn't going to ruin your career. Between welfare, WIC, and food stamps, they will use the system to their advantage. Crime was here before you came here.'

"I sit there and say, 'You don't know a fuckin' thing. You have no idea of what this job is about. Maybe you remember that grand larceny is extortion. Frankly, I was afraid to talk into that radio. I was so naive I didn't know how to write a summons. No one knows anything. Now I know the job pretty well. That doesn't mean you're going to know everything. You're absolutely clueless. Do not be afraid to ask questions. Please come to me. No matter how stupid it is, I've heard it and I will give you the right answer. That's what we're here for.'

"It's a civil service job," Patrick continues. "The starting salary for cops in New York City is thirty-one thousand dollars. I don't think you become a criminal out of this job. There are forty thousand cops. You round up forty thousand people and a percentage of them . . . I still think that the integrity of police is above the rest of society. You have to remember that this Police Department is larger than some countries' armies.

"Why should the people of the City of New York think that the Police Department is a whole bunch of corrupt thugs? Every day they put their faith in us."

As powerful as the PBA is perceived to be, not every cop at the 23rd Precinct supports the union or its delegates. One veteran cop grumbles, "What would happen if I decided not to join the union? I don't really have a choice. I could negotiate better deals myself."

"The PBA—they've been bought and paid for," says another. "It's old-time bullshit. They only take care of their own. Here you see them put in a deal and everyone hears about it. They got no balls. They have the perception of being well connected. 'We must be there—you need us.' If a guy who is the PBA delegate doesn't like you, then you're fucked."

"People who are delegates should work patrol," the veteran cop insists. "PBA delegates are in details [special crime units]. They are protecting their positions. There should be representation at all levels. The role of the PBA needs to be defined a little more clearly. People don't understand that you have the option of saying something. A PBA representative cannot be held to any standard of honesty. They have to advance the best line possible. They can't come in and say, 'This guy is dirty.' I firmly believe some people give tradeoffs with payback. Guys have to build up credibility with them."

"Does the PBA run the command?" one cop challenges. "No. People who [think] that expect different treatment. They have no idea of what a union is. Membership doesn't have a say of what goes on. They're too busy—the PBA is a big political machine. They control a lot of money in the city. They decide where to invest funds. They have some amount of clout. But day-to-day rank-and-file union organization? No. Maybe years ago, but it's not that way anymore. I don't think much of the old-boy network. These guys have been around forever—since the seventies—in some capacity. There's a lot of nepotism. Guys have no clue that they should have a right of say. They have no work experience.

"Most cops are intelligent people who accept where they are, where they want to be. They don't see how important it is to have some sort of understanding of what each one of their contracts does for them. They're so spread out. No one knows when the contract expires. The sergeant's contract, the captain's contract expire at different times.

"Our only representation is the PBA. So we're stuck with them," he concludes.

One cop recalls working in the 30th Precinct, known as the "Dirty Thirty," where cops were arrested for shaking down drug dealers. "In the Three-oh, one of the delegates organized a summons falsification scheme, where guys would write down twenty-five summonses when giving out two, back in 1992. As a result, every cop and supervisor in the precinct had to verify the amount of summonses. If cops feel that they've been put upon by management, they can orchestrate things. The PBA will never say that they sanctioned it.

"One delegate ran that precinct for a while," he says of the 30th Precinct. " 'Vote for him or your car will be damaged.' Everyone parks in that garage; everyone was concerned. There was a huge pile of beer bottles there. There was drinking in the radio cars. There was money to be made. I remember seeing a radio car one time, an unmarked car behind his. [Marked] money came out of the car window. It was a setup. They were trying to get rid of [marked] money that was being checked by Internal Affairs.

"Cops got clothes cleaned free. Cops wore beepers. Cops are not supposed to be wearing beepers. No one's allowed to carry beepers. What do you need a beeper for? If you need it, call the command and get the message. It became an old-boys network."

Police Woman

Officer Tara Casey sweeps around the edges of three green metal lockers with an old broom and throws out a discarded piece of Christmas wrapping paper. "The women are filthier than the men sometimes," she says with disgust, surveying the 23rd Precinct's women's locker room. It's crowded with bunk beds, lockers, shoes, towels, and heavy wooden benches manufactured in an upstate prison. She often scrubs down the bathroom with ammonia and cleans sinks, stalls, and showers. "I can't help it. I'm a neat freak and I have to work here eight hours a day."

Casey, tending to an ailing mother with Alzheimer's, works her own hours under an arrangement with her captain. Recognizing the stress of her mother's illness, and Casey's seniority and ex-perience, he allows her to arrive late at night, to work an impro-vised tour, handling paperwork and other matters inside the stationhouse. Casey has served twenty-two years as a police officer in Brooklyn and Manhattan.

She confides: "The worst was being shot at, seeing other cops shot and killed, having to search a dead body and having an arm come off in your hand. Or sitting there with your own emotions when you're scared shitless.

"My first week on the job—this was the era of being shot at—I'm laying on top of dog shit and human pee in the gutter, being shot at from a storefront. I was scared shitless, except that shit was under me."

Born in Woodside and raised in Rego Park, Queens, Casey worked as a secretary at the Bricklayers Union, took bets at OTB (Off Track Betting) and worked as a cocktail waitress at night before joining the New York City Police Department. "I was a go-go dancer," she says, a tall, no-nonsense woman with a round, pleasant face, brown eyes, and an infectious laugh. "These were the days of *Laugh-In*. I danced in go-go boots and a micro-mini in a cage at the opening of clubs. I wanted to be a professional dancer. I did the Swim, the Chicken, the Twist, the Frug, the Fly, all of those dances. I didn't want a regular job. I was rebelling against society."

She took the policewoman's test in 1969. "The Police Depart-ment was a ways from anything that I had in mind. I was going to be dancing on stage. I remember the day of the test. I was out all night and I was hungover."

The Police Department had a quota for women. She was hired four years later when there was an opening. Casey's career began in Bushwick, Brooklyn, October 1973, at the 83rd Precinct, a community of poor and working-class blacks, Hispanics, and Ital-ians. "They were fearfully respectful," she remembers. "It would

be the rarity if someone talked shit to a cop, because they knew
they would get a beating. You wouldn't dare. He'd beat the living
crap out of you."

On her first day, "A fellow that I knew, Tom, a sergeant in the
precinct, brought me into the office and introduced me to the
captain. 'She's going to be reporting here Monday,' he said to him.
I reached out my hand to shake the captain's as he stood up. He
said, 'I don't want you here. I don't need you here. I'm going to
make sure you die here.'

"I was scared out of my mind. I thought I *was* going to die. I
know I didn't cry. Tom apologized to me outside. I think even he
was floored by this. I thought my life was over. 'What did I get
myself into?' " she asked—still incredulous over her treatment. "I
heard about discontent among the guys, negatives about men and
women working together, wives picketing police headquarters,
saying that it was unsafe to work with female cops.

"The captain put me on the worst footpost. I was just so con-
sumed about not getting into trouble. No one would talk to you.
Tradition back then, if you're a rookie you're not spoken to for
years. You didn't ride in a car for five years. Complicate that by
being the most hated thing on earth—a woman."

New cops had no formal lockerroom and there was no separate
women's bathroom at the 83rd Precinct.

"They gave us an old, tiny little room and we painted it. We
had to share a bathroom with the men. Eventually, there were
about eight women among three hundred men. I just wanted to
get through the tours so I could cry. As soon as I got a block away
and turned, I would sob. It wasn't the street that scared me; it
was the cops that scared me. It was humiliating and degrading.
They'd say, 'We hate you, you shouldn't be here. You're useless.'
It wasn't just me. It was the whole atmosphere. They were primed
and supported by the PBA. They wanted our dues. They didn't
want us.

"When we were out on jobs, they'd push and shove you out of the way. They wanted to be in control. Once I was shoved halfway across a kitchen. When we got downstairs, I told the guy I was riding with and he said, 'Why are you telling me? Tell him. This is the street. You take care of business.' From then on, if someone said something, I asked them why and told them not to do it again. Then it became easier. I had a nightstick thrown at me in the muster room. It was a test. They all tested rookies as a way to drive you away. Are you going to cry or run to the boss? No one's going to fight your battles.

"One man was forced to work with me in a radio car. He came out with a tirade of expletives. 'I'm not opening the fuckin' car door for you. Are we supposed to be gentlemen? If you don't like the way I'm fuckin' talking, it's too fuckin' bad.' I said, 'Hey, look, I don't use curse words. As long as you're not calling me these names, I don't care what you say.' "

Officer Casey recalls carrying a severed head in a plastic bag, and delivering a baby as the umbilical cord strangled it, while her male partner—unable to handle the pressure—ran out of the apartment. She reminisces about rolling in gutters as bullets whizzed around her.

When she wasn't on foot, she worked in a black-and-white patrol car, with no power steering, no air conditioning, no portable police radio. "It was so hot that I was changing my summer shirt three or four times a day. At one point, I owned thirty-four shirts." She laughs.

The Police Department hadn't given much thought to the role of women back then. "We had to wear a skirt with stockings and heels, and a little cross tie. We also carried a shoulder bag," she says, shaking her head in disbelief. "I walked a footpost in a skirt. I would go through pantyhose climbing ladders and climbing over rooftops every day. I was used to people looking up my skirt. We wore a navy style hat that cost twenty-five dollars. A man's cost four dollars. We didn't have a choice. We were issued these things. What the hell *were* we supposed to do with these handbags?"

Casey filled in for six months in the Anti-Crime Unit, dressing as a decoy, until she and almost every other woman in the Police Department were laid off in the middle of 1975 during New York City's fiscal crisis. When Casey was rehired in December 1977, she was assigned to the 23rd Precinct.

"I remember a cop blown away with a shotgun. I don't want to talk about that. I can't," she says, looking away. "Back then cops were getting killed all the time. I remember going to a job and a cop was shot through a door. The aftermath—everybody was responding. There were ambushes all the time. On One Hundred Tenth Street, the FALN [Armed Forces of National Liberation, a Puerto Rican pro-independence group] placed a bomb in a building. At that time, the Twenty-third Precinct covered the south side; the Two-five, the north side. They were after the Two-five for some reason. They called in a job and a bomb went off. The cop, he was blinded. He had an eye blown out. What did he ever do to anyone?"

Casey partnered with a sergeant—nicknamed "T"—as his driver. The two were busy supervising and responding to job after job every evening. When work ended, she became a frequent guest at his holiday dinners and family celebrations. "He was great to work with," she says. "He treated me like an equal."

Like many older women who have paid their dues, complaints by younger women about working conditions seem almost incomprehensible. "Now you'll find a lot of women doing inside work or giving out summonses. They get forty-five thousand dollars a year to be meter maids. And they're complaining. Years ago, a guy had twenty-five years and he got that job because he earned it. Within six months, some women are doing this. I was doing patrol. If you're working inside, you're a fifty-thousand-dollar-a-year secretary," she says. "They should make the test harder and you'd get more aggressive females. This female cop that I knew was an ass-kisser. She'd go shopping for the sergeant and she'd make his lunch. If she were a man, she'd be ostracized. A man couldn't do that. The sergeant would be looking to dump him. With the female, it was all right.

"I find it absolutely absurd," she says angrily, "after I broke my ass [along] with all the females who broke down barriers. Now, some females are complaining and whining and raising those political-type excuses because they're incompetent. I think of what I had to take, to be minutely accepted. It wasn't acceptance, it wasn't tolerance. Now they've got it made. Any whining piss-ass woman would have been chop meat back then. They never would have made the Academy. I just cannot stand some of the women in this Department. This shit is behind us and we can deal with anything else. They don't know what 'shit hit the fan' means."

Sergeant Matt Kennedy notices the squat figure of a cop with oversized hips standing on the corner of 104th Street and Second Avenue. He drives up to her.

"How many summons do you have?" he asks her sternly. Since Grace Pineda has failed the driving portion of the Police Academy requirements, she is assigned to a footpost.

"Six," she replies.

"We're entering that stage again," he says, irritably. "This is three months. You haven't made any more. You've got to write more summonses. Listen up. I will call you and you will come over and write," he orders.

He speeds away, his foot stamping the gas pedal.

"And I'm supposed to answer the questions: What are you doing about this? What are you doing to correct her activity?" Kennedy says, perturbed. "I don't expect her to chase cars, she's not prolific enough to operate a patrol car. I'm not looking for someone to be a star. She's either improperly trained or just so fuckin' stupid. It's scary that you would trust someone like her with a gun. I'm amazed! I don't know if it disillusions me or scares the hell out of me. I see her bailing out or fucking up or we have a bigger disaster. I'm shocked that she made it out of the fuckin' Academy.

"A lot of people say she's crazy, that she doesn't know what's going on. It's borderline scary. She's a nice person. She's just not very bright. If you ask her to bake a cake, she'd probably do it. On this job, a lot of shit gets pushed around. If you're a fuckup and a nice fuckup, people find a spot for you. If you're a good-looking fuckup and you're a female and you don't have an attitude—if you're just stupid and naive and have no fuckin' clue— you don't want to put your pen to hurt her. Someone would review it and can her. But she'll still get pushed around until they find something—maybe another Hispanic female—to work with her. They might bond and be put together in a car. It's frightening."

"I come from a different batch of people," Kennedy says. "Everyone had a brain."

Several cops at the 23rd Precinct are single mothers raising sons and daughters on their own. A few diligently study for the sergeant's test. Mothers compare notes on breast feeding and babysitters. Two women compare notes on who they've had affairs with. One lives in fear of an abusive ex-husband. Another is looking for a husband, attest four male cops who have slept with her. One had a mother who was a heroin addict.

Sometimes women partner together, because men refuse to work with them.

Officer Grace Pineda dropped out of high school when she was sixteen, obtaining her high-school-equivalency diploma a year later. "For three-and-a-half years, I was a housewife. I was on public assistance for four-and-a-half years. All the struggle, all the torture in the Academy," she says, adjusting her too-small hat and too-tight pants. "I'm asthmatic. I get that wheezing. I used to get shin splints. My mother would tape my legs every day. I looked like a mummy, but it worked. In the Police Academy, it was horrendous. I really needed the benefits because of my daughter. The only good thing about the Police Academy was the Medicaid. Being a police officer is pretty cool."

Two older women cops are dubbed "Tootsie and Mrs. Doubtfire" and "the Golden Girls." Mrs. Doubtfire had shot and paralyzed her EMS boyfriend, insisting that she was a victim of domestic violence. "What if she gets a flashback?" asks one concerned cop who keeps his distance.

The second half of the Golden Girls is Donna Hernandez, a former truck driver, who worked with Mrs. Doubtfire for several days because no one else was available. "She has no clue. No one will work with her. I'm worried about my safety," Hernandez admits. "Sometimes it's better to work alone."

Another cop worries about Hernandez, too: "Donna Hernandez never followed me, never ran. I thought I was by myself. She's a great person, but that experience changed me. I wanted to work with someone else. Your partner is the most important person you work with. I run left, he runs left. It was over, that was it. I wouldn't work with her again."

Miranda Mays works in the complaint room. "My father wanted me to be a stronger person, to be able to take care of myself. He felt that I would learn to take care of myself and make quick decisions." Mays is an attractive black woman so small and thin at 110 pounds that the equipment on her gun belt dangles together. She complains about working inside the stationhouse and not on the street: "Inside the house is not really by choice. I was inside so much that I learned the paperwork and I'm the only person who knows the stuff. Every once in a while I go out," she says, not unhappily. "A lot of people who work here—being that I don't come out that much—they're a little afraid. They never actually have a chance to work with me. I feel like I have to be accepted, to do something drastic like grabbing a collar. Some women are accepted because they are good-looking. I would like to be accepted as a person."

"You're not going to fit in on their terms," says Donna Hernandez. "You're different. If you're a hard worker, you'll get credit. You really have to have a highly, highly developed sense of humor. The big difference is the men don't sweat the small stuff. Women do. I find that I have to stop."

"My personal opinion," offers one male cop. "I don't think women belong on this job, but they're here and we have to deal with them. There are women who are true heroes, but for every one, there are ten to fifteen who would crawl under a desk. There's also men on this job who don't belong here. There's nothing I can do to change that. Equal rights for everyone. They're here to stay and we have to accept it. I just think that having a female partner is a disadvantage. I'd rather go out there with a big guy than a small female. I'd feel safer."

One female cop who is gay transferred to another precinct rather than endure torment by her male counterparts. "She used to get personal mail here," says a second female cop. "Someone opened her mail and stuck it on the bathroom wall. They put an M-80 in the toilet. Why are you blowing up the toilet? You have to carry yourself with respect. She had an attitude and she showed that they were bothering her. It fed them; she showed her weakness. They would call her 'dyke' over the radio.

"I'm gay, also. I had a hard time, too. The men were trying to date me. Everyone was betting to see who was going to get me first. If you come up and ask me, I'll acknowledge myself. One of the guys just asked me and I said, 'Yes, it's true. No problem. I get along.'"

Sergeant Colombo gripes: "You ain't got a fuckin' female cop that's worth shit. They're not physically capable or mentally capable. Too many fuckin' women cause fuckin' grief."

"We hold ourselves back," admits Donna Hernandez. "A lot of girls have kids and the kids come first. Many don't want the stress and strain of not knowing when you're going home. You'll find a Monday-through-Friday job because it's more important to be home with your kids. We women have so many different agendas. All this shit is so complicated."

One female sergeant was called a "cunt" by several male cops she supervised. "I'm treated as an equal," she says. "If I give an order, you take it. I don't care what's written about me in the bathroom. If someone fucks up, I'll yell at you. Deal with my yelling. I try and do it as diplomatically as possible. We'll straighten it out. As a woman you have to work twice as hard to get half the respect. They've accepted me for what I am."

"I worked with a female partner," says one male sergeant, "and I loved her like a sister."

Anita Perez decided to become a cop after watching television—*Charlie's Angels*. Four years a cop, she still hasn't quite found her place, alternating between coyness and vulgarity, flirting with the men and putting down the women, and sometimes the opposite. Perez once looked at a rare roast beef sandwich and declared, "It looks like a Kotex." One male cop reluctantly admits being afraid of her. "She was all over me in the car," he says, nervously. "She wanted me to sleep with her. I'm petrified. What am I supposed to do?" Ultimately, he transferred to another precinct, tormented by the possibility of repercussions if he refused.

Perez's patrol car screeches to the corner of 109th and Lexington as she and her latest partner pull over to complete some paperwork during the four-to-twelve tour. A tiny light flickers in a window.

"That's a crack vial being lit," notes Perez. A matronly-looking black woman, accompanied by a young boy, approaches the car. Perez mutters to herself, "What does this fuckin' bitch want?" The woman, polite and concerned, says that a wino threw wine on her eight-year-old son. "I want the man arrested," she demands.

"Ma'am, is your son hurt?" Perez asks brusquely. "You can fill out a harassment complaint form. Let me speak to your son. Where did he hit you?" The son doesn't answer.

"Tell him that he hit you," insists his mother.

"Ma'am, you can't do that," Perez says, sounding irritated. "We can't do anything."

The stories are legion of frightened female cops refusing to get out of their patrol cars on dangerous jobs and locking the car doors. Male cops complain that women aren't fast enough, aren't strong enough, and don't back them up. A woman like Anita Perez who can handle herself out on the streets is complimented and admired when she exhibits the same qualities the men admire.

"I didn't come to do a man's job," she says. "I came to work in the Police Department. Your chances of changing it are slim to none. You can change yourself. A lot of toughness is an act. A lot of it is physical appearance. A woman has to be an aggressive cop in order to get respect. Once she gets pregnant and can't go into the street, then it's all over. The men don't want to hear about it. If she gets pregnant, and she was aggressive before then, then at least they can say, 'Well—she *used* to be a good cop.' "

Perez, who lived in the Bronx and Manhattan before moving to upstate New York, owns both a sewing machine and a lawn mower. "People say that I'm a bitch at work but different at home."

"You're very popular these days. It must be your new makeup," chides her partner, Will Montanez.

"It's almost like a survival type of thing," Perez says of him. "Will is the most levelheaded. In the beginning, I had no partners. They wouldn't let you establish a partner system. You had the uncomfortable experience of riding with someone else's partner.

Sometimes you'd have nothing in common. Sometimes we really didn't have nothing to talk about. What the fuck am I going to say? I'm still fairly young. I still have that need for the action, the dangerous things thrown in my face. I race all around the precinct, up and down.

"It's not easy being a girl on this job. In the beginning, it was pretty tough. Guys have to go through that macho process. They see who gets the dates. That's only if you're a decent-looking girl. Out in the street, it's a different story." Perez, a sturdy five-three, with a bouncing ponytail, looks everyone straight in the eye. "From what I've seen, Arabs are pretty respectful. I've never had an incident with them," she says. "Black males fight you, perps fight you. They have bad attitudes. It all depends on whether you want to get your head bashed in. Most of the time Will never does any of the talking. It's just the way it's worked out. Sometimes with heated arguments people see cops and they see male cops. They think with me it's passive and they're all wrong. You have to protect people's rights. I don't think civilians who are carrying guns should have that protection. Suppose you're out on patrol and you see five guys hanging out. For what purpose? You don't know what these people are planning. I've approached a group of five men before, in uniform. It's scary. You can feel the blood pumping.

"Cops think that women cops are fuckin' lazy. And women do become complacent," she says. "I see no room in my life for babies. If it does happen, I wouldn't do something to get rid of it. I'd probably be upset for a while because I wasn't ready. I'll take all the tests," Perez says, referring to promotional tests leading to sergeant, lieutenant, and captain. "Once I'm up there, then you can go fine up to menopause. Maybe sergeant, maybe not. You can't move up being a young mommy. I don't care what people say about me. I just come here to do my job."

It was Perez who earned Cop-of-the-Month honors by arresting a man wanted in the shooting of a Mafia boss. She and Montanez spotted the shooter's car and pulled him over. "I was so scared," she says. "I was shaking. I didn't know what this man was going to do." He surrendered without any fuss. "I didn't know much about him. We were looking for the car. They said, 'Northbound on Park.' Will said, 'The guy's not on Park.' I told Will, 'He has to be on Third.' Third Avenue has three or four lanes. All cars are just flowing up the street. We came down One Hundred Tenth Street, made a left turn, and Will spotted half of the license plate and we stopped him. You hear the guy is wanted for a shooting at Lenox Hill Hospital. You don't think nothing of it, but when you have the person in front of you, you start to freak out.

"I said, 'Willy, if anything happens, shoot first, ask questions later.' Every cop has different ways of doing things. Some will go up with a gun in their hand, by way of dealing with it. I know my partner is there with his gun out. If I pull up with my gun out, then the guy's going to know something's up. He could think I'm there for a broken tail light. He'll be scared and could start firing at me. At this point, I'm still passive. I make sure Will gets out with a gun. I go up to the driver's side. I told him to put his hands out where I can see them. I give him a toss. I ask him to step out. He had nothing on him. He could feel the nervousness in my hands. I told him to go by Will and we tore apart the car there. I know I was nervous. Will asked me if I was scared. 'No,' I said, 'get the fuck out of here!' Twenty-five police cars came from everywhere. It was almost annoying. So many people show up, it becomes confusion."

Detective Jennie Rodriguez remembers one of her first days on patrol as a cop: "The woman called for the police. I went with my partner, who was a female. The woman said, 'You're not the police. You're not a man.' The call never came in that she was a bigot. I said, 'Fuck her.' I was shocked. Your job is to help people. Some people don't want to be helped. They treat you like garbage when you try and help them. I showed her my radio. She said, 'I want a real officer.' If I wasn't good enough, she wasn't getting anyone else. So I left."

A cop: "An officer who speaks Spanish, they try to relate [to] a little more. Not speaking Spanish, guys have a helluva time understanding. But women are not accepted by them as a form of authority, no matter how forceful—to the point of drawing her revolver. Now you have a frustrated police officer and four drunk Mexicans not listening to her. Women are there to serve them. They don't want to take orders from a female. Their culture doesn't allow for females to give orders or talk down to them. It's a culture barrier. With some men, there's no bullshit and no talking back. Some of it was down-and-out brutality. But you had the respect that you don't have now."

Detective Jennie Rodriguez, the only woman in the Robbery-in-Progress unit, drives the gray undercover car up Third Avenue on her way to the Bronx to pick up a witness. "The bad guys know what these cars look like. They spot these freaking cars," she complains.

A Puerto Rican woman who favors suits and drives a sharp red sports car, she is the daughter of a farmer from Puerto Rico. She thought she would become a furrier, but her sister convinced her that she should become a cop like her husband. She first worked as a store detective and then as a court interpreter before taking the Police Department test.

"I get my respect, I do my work. I'm not here doing my hair or my nails to get attention or shit. I'm one of the guys. Period. You got to be one of the guys, you got to be. You're there to protect their back. If you can't, you're worthless to them. It's hard. There are some lazy bitches. They're just lazy. A lot of women are married and have kids. The kids are in school or at a day care center. They'd rather be at home with the kids. I don't have to worry about that. I'm not married, no kids."

In East Harlem, Hispanic men call out to women. "What's this 'Mommy' shit?" complains Rodriquez. "I have to set them straight. I'm not their 'Mommy.' " One black female cop was called "Sister" by a black man she was arresting. "Sister?" she retorted. "Are you sitting across from me at the dinner table?! I'm not your sister."

Detective Rodriguez was once called a woman, not a detective, by a man who robbed and beat his wife. "This guy hit his wife and took her jewelry. I went to talk to him," she says, still sounding annoyed. "I started to say, 'Yeah, I don't take sides.' I told him, 'I'm an officer.' 'Woman, my ass,' he said. 'You're a woman.' I was so pissed off. 'You robbed her, you hit her!' I told him. 'It has nothing to do with whether I'm a woman or a man. I'm doing my job. That's what I got a shield for. I would be on her side if she was a thief.' They think you take sides," she says, shaking her head. "I've had perps call me homo, 'That fuckin' homo hooked me up.' I don't care about these people, because I don't have to work with them. I don't take shit from nobody."

Rodriguez's witness, who promised to be home, wasn't. So she returns to the 23rd Precinct.

"I've never seen such young kids," she says of the rookies. Rodriguez is forty-two and has been a cop since 1983. "It must be that I'm so freaking old. I took the test when I was twenty-nine. I take it more seriously. Every ten years I take it even more seriously.

"You know what's out there. You know you can get into trouble if you don't do the right thing. We went to a job during the summer. All the cars converged. A kid in uniform ran and stood on top of the car. I said that it was so unprofessional. Is he stupid or what? You wouldn't do it in front of the captain. You don't give a shit, you have no respect. You wouldn't do it on Thirty-fourth Street.

"Then one time shots were fired. I remember the guys laughing and carrying on. You're supposed to be professional people instead of like, jerks. That's why there are these training sessions, like, sensitivity training, every morning. It used to be once a month. Because of complaints coming in, you don't know who's out there watching. You have to conduct yourself like everyone out there is taking notes."

"These guys are very nice," she says of her colleagues, but she complains of feeling isolated. Each member of the RIP unit has a turn at catching cases, which consists of sitting in the office, and handling complaints. They all consider it torture. "They're very good. These guys—even though they're not your partners—you work with them all the time. You'll go out with them. I'm always the odd man out because I'm the only female and I'm an odd female, but they really don't want to hang out with me. Men are always doing this or that—talking about women, looking at girls. They don't want me out there. Why go out with me when you have another guy, another buddy? I would probably do the same thing. It makes it easier. I can't stand waiting around for a robbery report. This is for lazy people. I still have a lot of energy. I love all that shit, running around. If something comes in, you handle it and come in so that it's not just sitting here. I don't feel like no detective sitting here all fuckin' day. I want to work a good case, staying with it from beginning to end. It's my case. But that's in the movies."

Still, she put in a transfer to the Sixth Precinct in Greenwich Village. "That's my turf. That's home for me. I identify with these people. A lot of people come in and say, 'Oh, I know you're gay.' Even the perps. A lot of people don't like that. If they don't like gay people, they'll hold back. They don't want you to come to their house and tell you their business. Most people in the Sixth Precinct, they know who you are and they won't talk to a straight cop who hates them. A lot of men find it easier to talk to guys than to me. To them, I'm not a detective because I'm not a man.

"I can't think about their problem. I'm just arresting them for someone else's complaint. They're being arrested for what they did. I can't get emotionally involved. I'd get nuts. You can't function. You'd end up feeling sorry for everyone and you can't do your job. The victims are a whole different thing sometimes. Nothing moves me here. But the perp with the elevator pattern, he robbed a lady in a wheelchair. He stopped her and he hit her. She wasn't going to do anything. She couldn't. She could hardly talk. And he took her chain. She's in her early sixties. She had a stroke. You couldn't make out her words. They had to get a microphone. She couldn't get up the stairs. She had to walk with a metal cane. Her leg was all twisted. This woman went through hell for this bastard. No one got their property back. When the trial was over, only the property from the people who he robbed the day he got arrested was given back. He took it all to different pawn shops. They melt that shit down. You know what I'm saying?"

A tearful Chinese girl from Chinatown comes in and sits on a chair next to Rodriguez's desk. "She came up here to cop some reefer," Detective Mendez explains. "Some guy bitch-slapped her and took her stuff."

"You should call her mother. Look her up in the phone book," offers Rodriguez. "How old is she? Fourteen?"

Officer Vicky Torres, twenty-six, joined the New York City Police Department after receiving a bachelor's degree from John Jay College of Criminal Justice in June 1993. She lives in the Bronx, her partner in Queens. "I'm not sure why I became a cop. I haven't been able to answer that question myself. I like to work outside.

I hate being in an office. I grew up in a very crime-ridden neigh-borhood in the Bronx, in the housing projects. I guess that had an impact. I know how these people feel, trying to make it better for yourself with all this crime. I like the excitement and being able to see a lot of different things. I think I've seen every parade in New York City.

"I used to love doing dangerous things like running up fire escapes. As you get older, you realize you could kill yourself. Now with my daughter, I have a different perspective," she says.

Tall and wiry with her dark hair neatly pulled back into a ponytail, Torres is just one of two women on patrol during the day tour. "At first, it was kind of rough," she says. "The guys didn't know where I was coming from. They don't like women who don't like to work. They put you more to the test than men who aren't working. You have to assert yourself and not let the guys step all over you. It's self-respect. You have to learn how to carry yourself or it gets out of hand. Yeah, you have to be a little bit of a bitch. The ideal female is one who works in the street and who doesn't become a man.

"It was an accumulation of incidents," Torres says of her ac-ceptance. "It's very hard. They saw that I wasn't afraid to do my job. But I think it's over a period of time; you're under the watchful eye."

Torres looks at the latest headlines highlighting a corruption investigation in another precinct. "With corruption, I feel really disgusted," she says. "The honest cop risks his safety and his job, and it's a slap in the face. It makes our job harder. It's just dis-gusting. You get disgusted."

The Numbers Racket

The Knapp Commission charged that half of New York's cops were corrupt, and that henceforth only narcotics officers could make narcotics arrests. Cops were told to stay out of stores. Probationary officers straight out of the Academy were segregated from senior cops for fear that the impressionable newcomers would be tainted by the contact. At the same time, the newer officers missed the benefit of working with experienced officers. The Department, however, was determined to truncate the corruption even if it meant walling off the fledging cops.

During the fifties and sixties, entire divisions of the Police Department, known as "pads," had been regularly paid off to overlook gambling and prostitution. Posts were sold. In some instances, a $1,000 payoff to a roll-call cop netted a regular seat in a patrol car. From there on a cop was forced to make $500 to $700 per month in additional payoffs.

Cops began losing their streets in the 1970s, when a violent crime was committed every 36 seconds. There was no money for new equipment, recruitment, or the training of new officers. Younger cops, and most of the women hired, were laid off. The average age of a cop was thirty-eight.

Precincts were closed and reopened and operated with fewer patrol cars. Cops demonstrated in front of precinct houses and in front of Gracie Mansion, the mayor's home. In 1976, the FALN terrorist group, which advocated Puerto Rican independence, bombed the historic Fraunces Tavern, killing four and injuring forty-four. Bombs were found in department stores. Combating crime was a scattered and disorganized affair.

The City's more corporate and organized crime fighting strategies can be traced to a philosophy articulated by James Q. Wilson and George Kelling in a 1982 *Atlantic Monthly* magazine article outlining their "broken windows theory" that neighborhood disorder—including drunks, panhandling, youth gangs, prostitution, and other seemingly smaller urban problems—creates fear among residents and attracts criminals. And just as a broken window may indicate that nobody cares about a building and lead to more serious vandalism, disorderly behavior also signals that nobody cares about a community and leads to more serious disorder and crime. The new Transit Police commissioner, William Bratton, adopted the theory and applied it, beginning with the New York Transit System. The idea seemed to be borne out when they discovered that people arrested for jumping turnstiles were often carrying boxcutters, knives, guns, and were wanted on outstanding warrants.

Later hired as police commissioner of the entire city, Bratton increased the firepower of cops from the standard .38 to the 9mm semi-automatic pistol, in order to keep up with weaponry brandished by criminals. He added more cops on bicycles. He coordinated efforts of different units, noting that crime (especially drug dealing) didn't take a day off on Saturdays and Sundays when most cops were off. One of his deputies, Jack Maple, came up with the idea of maps examining the seven major crimes—including homicide, assault, rape, burglary, and auto theft—and deployed cops accordingly. A tough new management criterion was introduced, holding precinct captains accountable for their turf. At monthly meetings they would be pressed for results and strategies to combat crime in their neighborhoods. With fewer guns on the street, it made sense that there was less opportunity for people to shoot one another. Bratton targeted drug activity both inside buildings and out on the street. Police confiscated and traced guns found on drug dealers, and coordinated their efforts with federal and state agencies. Precinct cops worked in plainclothes, and cops were able to make arrests seven days a week, twenty-four hours a day. Before Bratton, there had been no system to identify and track domestic violence; he developed domestic-violence incident reports. In keeping with the "broken windows theory," the Police Department focused on quality-of-life issues—boom boxes, squeegee people, street prostitutes, public drunks, panhandlers, reckless bicyclists, and graffiti.

The New York City Police Department, the Transit Police, and the Housing Police were merged into one in 1995. ("It's not a merger—it's a hostile takeover," complained Housing Police Lieutenant Johnny Broderick.) An enhanced 911 system was installed, which instantly traced a call. Under a new program starting in February 1999, anyone arrested for driving while under the influence of illegal drugs could have their car seized. If a suspect was convicted, his car was auctioned off.

Commanding officers had to report the details of each homicide and each spike in crime as if they were personally responsible. The pursuit of better statistics at the 23rd Precinct, which had no known prostitution problem, resulted in female cops being ordered to go undercover and catch men soliciting prostitutes. A few were.

"I don't like this," complained one female officer. "I'm not dressing up like a whore for the Police Department. That's not my job."

Cops argue that New York City will never be crime free, but the mayor presses the police commissioner to reduce crime levels, who passes the pressure on to his chiefs, then on to commanding officers, captains, lieutenants, detectives, sergeants, and on down to the cops—the men and women in the street. With crime reduced, cops often find themselves chasing the seemingly insignificant things. Instead of an armed drug dealer, they're ticketing a dog owner who hasn't picked up after his dog. "This is embarrassing," complains a street cop. "No wonder the public doesn't like us."

"Morale is at an all-time low," a PBA delegate insists. "In fourteen years, I've never seen anything like it. How much of this can you take? I ain't doing shit."

Approaches have changed; instead of focusing on the individual burglar, the Police Department looks at the bigger picture and goes after the source—fences who traffic in stolen goods, chop shops, and local drug gangs. After the killings at Colorado's Columbine High School in May of 1999, the Department compiled blueprints of all city schools so that emergency units would know their layouts in a crisis.

There are more cops but fewer of them on the beat. The 23rd Precinct's ten cops in five cars has been reduced to six cops in three cars on the four-to-twelve shift. Cops, including the graduating classes of rookies, have been transferred to specialized units to concentrate on the drug trade.

*   *   *

Reports are documented. Categories of crimes and their locations are noted, patterns tracked and crime-fighting strategies adapted. Crime statistics have plunged. However, there are problems with the new approach. If a crime is not reported to the Police Department, then it's considered not to have occurred.

"A lot of people here don't call the police," says one cop in the 23rd Precinct. "They tell you nothing when you ring the apartment."

A number of East Harlem residents are illegal immigrants, living in fear of being deported. Unaware that, if they are a victim of a crime, they cannot be deported, they remain afraid that any contact with a government agency will reveal their secret and result in expulsion. "They are victims of crimes not reported," says one cop. "They're all victims of crime until they settle in and work their way out of lower status. Really, there is no answer. People are always going to commit crimes for one reason of another. Other people are [going to be] afraid."

Citizens are more aware that they can sue their police departments. Twenty-eight-point-three million dollars was paid out in settlements in 1998 regarding police action, compared to $12.4 million in 1991. The number of suits alleging some form of police misconduct climbed from 1,335 in 1988 to 2,105 in 1999, a jump of nearly 58 percent. Cops mistakenly smashed down a door to an elderly couple's Bronx apartment in June 1997 with a battering ram. Cops based their information on an informant's tip that the home was the business office of a cocaine dealer. The couple won a $200,000 settlement from the city. A woman alleged that a detective hit her with a karate chop and slapped her; she received a $120,000 settlement. A man was awarded $180,000 stemming from an incident in August of 1993 when he was nineteen years old. He said he was stopped on a Queens street by two cops investigating a burglary, who threw him to the sidewalk and beat him with a flashlight, smashing his front teeth. Lawsuits are filed steadily. From 1994 to the present, the City has paid out over $177 million in 3,500 police misconduct cases. Forty million dollars a year is the recent estimate, even as the number of claims continues to decrease. Since 1999 they decreased by 25 percent, from 2,386 claims in 1999 to 1,766 in fiscal 2000.

Cops face precinct reprimands and loss of vacation days. The more serious departmental trials can result in the loss of their jobs. Charges range from the serious to the ridiculous, from minor violations of the *Patrol Guide* to criminal acts. The District Attorney might decline to prosecute a case, but the level of proof is lower in the Department's Trial Room. "If a captain doesn't like you, he says, 'I'll bring you up on charges,' " says one former trial room judge. "That's the last thing an officer wants to happen. They might lose vacation days, and they're embarrassed and humiliated."

His cases included a cop not wearing his hat, one carrying a paper bag, another wearing a Mickey Mouse medallion, another wearing a mustache below the crack of the lip, rape and sodomy cases, discharging guns, equipment stolen from sporting goods stores, making false allegations, committing perjury, and the case of a detective who swindled an elderly widow out of gold and diamonds.

"I recommended dismissal. The detective lost his job," says the judge. But the power is with the police commissioner. "It all depends on what his pet peeve is at the moment. And if you know the right people. One cop was charged with making a false statement. I found him not guilty, the police commissioner found him guilty. He lost fifteen days vacation."

"The Police Department is a very vindictive place," complains one sergeant. "There is no rhyme or reason to this Department. What goes for one person doesn't go for the next."

*   *   *

Officer Walter James recalls an incident with a local politician who argued and fought with him over a motorcycle summons. The politician filed a complaint with the Civilian Complaint Review Board.

"I think he has an obligation, and I had an obligation to do my job. I had to subdue him," says James. "Sorry. Now, I couldn't have been promoted if I was eligible. You're open to investigation and to scrutiny. 'Some police officer beat me up.' What does 'unsubstantiated' mean to a cop who is twenty-two?"

"People think it's a form of retaliation," says Lieutenant Johnny Broderick, who has twenty-five years of experience. "The true test of the CCRB is what is *founded*. It could be unsubstantiated. [If] there is evidence but no way to prove it, it's classified as *unfounded*. Say, you're at a demonstration with two hundred people. Cops are behaving in a correct manner. The leader of the demonstration says to all two hundred, 'Let's all file civilian complaints attributed to this precinct.' It's not an accurate gauge. The Police Department takes complaints from everyone—from drunks, people just arrested. It's not an accurate gauge. This Department goes by numbers. They don't take into consideration the reason why."

"Who's going to admit that you called them an asshole?" asked one female cop. "Of course, you deny it. Are you going to admit that you hit someone?"

"Be it summer, winter, fall—all I am is a number, I'm a fuckin' number," says Sergeant Charlie Columbo. "They don't care."

Five hundred seventy-one officers have been killed in the line of duty in the Department's long history, two in 2000. That same year six more died by their own hand.

Midnights

Squad B consists of ten men and women of various shapes, sizes, and temperaments, standing shoulder to shoulder in the 23rd Precinct muster room, preparing for the midnight shift five nights a week. They are dressed in blue shirts, blue pants and blue hats, with 9mm handguns, nightsticks, bulletproof vests, and flashlights.

Every tour has a different character: the midnights, older and more experienced, are a mixture of husbands and fathers, single men and women. Beat cops, captains, special units, and administrative personnel are home in bed, leaving staffing and supervision at a minimum. This "occupying army," as many people call them, consists of nine cops and one sergeant in five patrol cars keeping the peace within the precinct's one square mile.

In the muster room is a former champion high-school swimmer. Officer Larry Rivera still has the sturdy, confident build of an athlete and, although thirty-six, he has a boyish face framed by short-cropped, dark hair and brown eyes. Rivera sighs with the exasperation of a father chasing after a toddler, as his younger, energetic, restless partner speeds around East Harlem with little concern for automobiles and pedestrians. A twenty-pound gun belt, a bulletproof vest, no air conditioning, nauseating fumes from the car's engine, and his partner do nothing to ease his irritability. Not as quiet and casual as he appears, Rivera quickly sizes up people, methodically asks questions in even tones, and looks them dead in the eye.

Next to him stands Marc Aliberti, a graduate of the Culinary Institute of America, and the son of a retired FBI agent, who has earned the nickname "Forrest Gump" because he runs everywhere. ("I was fascinated by this world. I realized I wanted to live this life. It was exciting to me. I made the decision at two-thirty in the morning. I got all the books and studied for the test. I studied my ass off and I took a pay cut for this.") Hyperactive and abrasive, every car making an illegal turn, every kid standing on a corner as a drug lookout, every man with a gun, he takes as a personal affront. Handling the street has been deciphered by Rivera, but it still frustrates and angers Aliberti.

The only two things these partners have in common are the pregnancies of their wives, a first for both, and their interest in home remodeling. Aliberti lives in Queens, Rivera out on Long Island.

"I'm moving upstate," declares Aliberti. "I want to get away from that feeling that no one cares about each other."

Five of the ten police officers on midnights can't stand each other.

With just two steady partners among them and the remainder alternating, their common thread is complaining. "He's too slow." "He's too aggressive." "She doesn't know what he's doing." "I can't stand working with him."

Eric the Swede, blond and blue-eyed, fixes cars and ecstatically celebrates the birth of his daughter after months of his wife's fertility treatments. Al Vaez, nicknamed "Stretch" for his long legs and Gumby-like physique, fills patrol cars with smoke from his endless cigarettes. Sean Flanagan, an avowed atheist, taught himself Russian and always wears his bulletproof vest, even at weddings. Mike Pettit used to patrol in Central Park armed with a pair of binoculars, a tour of duty so slow he had come to recognized individual squirrels on sight. Kenny Jefferson partners with Leticia Trinidad, who often goes home to pray after yet another young man is killed over drugs. Popp Perez chainsmokes and drinks beer in uniform at a local bodega while on his break. Sharon Sanders and Yvette Colon, who have cornered men with machine guns, complain that they receive little or no backup from their male counterparts.

Several men call the two female officers "hogs" and have scratched the word into the sergeant's desk with keys. Yvette Colon said she had earned their hatred because she has refused the daily and constant advances of Perez, a married man with two young children, promptly and thoroughly informing him of her lack of interest. When he persisted, she complained. "She didn't have to complain. Now she's got him in trouble," a cop grouses. "Hogs," he mutters, under his breath.

The officers stand side by side for inspection at roll call, answering as their names are called, jotting down the night's assignments, and listening to the sermons on what criminal or crimes to watch for. Aliberti scratches at a piece of Scotch tape on the wall, holding up Department doggerel, an untitled poem:

You're a liar, a cheat, a crook, you're told
You should go to jail for things you have stole.
It's now TAKE YOUR POSTS!: Wait, summonses are down.
Have a nice day, but again they're around.
Now you're primed for the streets, pumped to the max!
While the hypocrite scum prepare their attacks.
A wallet is left to be seen in plain view,
Their pulse is now throbbing, what will you do?
You open the wallet and out jumps a dollar,
Their hearts are now pounding, do they have a collar?
You now go for coffee, the world can see,
The shadow is lurking did you get it for free?
Respond to a job, "EDP* with a bat,"
The first thing you think of is, "Am I wearing a hat?"

New York City separates the haves and the have-nots at East
96th Street. Below 96th Street on the upper East Side, residents
get their teeth bonded, crowned, and implanted; they suffer from
bulimia, and pay fortunes to dermatologists and massage thera-
pists. Above 96th Street, missing teeth aren't often replaced. Residents utilize food stamps, Clearasil, and orders of protection. Most
don't own property, or pay a premium for apartments with a view,
and they don't live next door to celebrities. More likely they rent
subsidized apartments and live next door to a criminal on parole,
and order Chinese food from behind plexiglass, shoplift because
they're hungry, or sell the food to buy drugs. Even diapers are
shoplifted and sold for drugs.

At night in the 23rd, people are locked in while some get locked up.

"Here your next-door neighbor probably has committed a
crime," says Rivera. "You're more likely to live next door to some-

*Emotionally Disturbed Person

one who's been in jail for assault or murder or drugs. You're not going to find that in the Nineteenth Precinct."

The 19th, the neighborhood south of 96th Street, covers Bloomingdale's, upscale bars and boutiques, million-dollar townhouses, penthouses, apartments, nannies, teenagers in private schools, and ladies who lunch.

Says Rivera, "If you're poor, no one gives a shit. If you're black, no one cares. If you're white, it's a different story. The media lives on this. Money and celebrity make the news. If you know how to push the right buttons, you will get instant service."

In the fancier precincts, the class differences are obvious: cops are treated like servants and expected to protect residents from intruders. In East Harlem, and other poor, minority neighborhoods, the police protect residents from each other. Criminals see the police as their enemy.

Aliberti inches the car slowly through 109th Street, a block, cops say, where residents either live in fear of a politically connected drug dealer or are on his payroll. Aliberti stops the car abruptly and points to a precinct landmark—11 East 109th Street where, in 1992, cops from the Street Crime Unit and an undercover cop from the 23rd Precinct were shot during a gun battle in a case of mistaken identity.

"They were chasing a man in the building. The stairwell wasn't lit and cops shot at each other. The guy they were chasing didn't get hurt. Of course," he adds, caustically.

In winter, more people fight in apartments. In summer, on hot nights, residents escape their steamy apartments and go out onto sidewalks and fire escapes. Puerto Rican, Italian, and black neighbors bring beach chairs and plastic crates out to their cement beaches, and sometimes a cold beer. Women fan themselves with cheap fans from local ninety-nine-cent stores, and dogs lie silent on the hot pavement. Rats feast on garbage, leftovers, and old sofas left at the curb. They share the block with men drinking beer in front of bodegas or on street corners, gathering in small groups to exchange news and gossip and play the congas. *Casitas*, little houses built on forgotten property or on city land, remind Puerto Ricans of their hometowns. These small community centers, surrounded by yards of plants and flowers, dot the neighborhood; older women in housedresses and men in undershirts sit quietly outside, listening to the low buzz of a radio. Dominoes clack as they are slapped down. People talk.

Hot and sticky. No breeze. The steamy night air sizzles in a patrol car without air conditioning. The four-door Chevy is Aliberti and Rivera's office for the evening. Their hats, nightsticks, memo books, and a bottle of water go into the back seat. The two cops lean as close to their car windows as they can as they begin another shift.

It is ninety-five degrees outside. The mandatory Kevlar bulletproof vests add at least another ten.

"There is no fuckin' air conditioning in East Harlem!" Rivera shouts angrily, kicking the dashboard with his black boots.

They drive slowly through dark streets, hoping to catch an open fire hydrant. When they do, the cops allow cool water to spray them. They pass an occasional stray dog, and a child wandering the streets. A ten-year-old walking alone in the early morning hours is nothing unusual.

"Oh, Lord! I don't ask for much. Just give me some a.c.!" Rivera cries out.

On Park Avenue and 105th Street they pass a movie crew filming a scene about cops. A special truck pumps air conditioning into a rented storefront where actors play out their parts.

"Now, that's realistic," Rivera says, sarcastically, and yells out the window, "Send some in here!"

Aliberti jams on the brakes so quickly that Rivera braces himself against the dashboard. His partner leans out the car window. A dark-skinned black man with a black cap, bad posture, and no teeth, stands back in the shadows of Lexington Avenue and 104th Street. His clothes hang loosely over his tall, slouched frame, his hands deep in his pockets. Cocaine and heroin are big sellers in East Harlem, but since the policemen haven't witnessed drugs or money changing hands, they can't arrest him.

"Hey, dude!" Aliberti calls out from the car. "Whatya got there?"

"What do you expect a black man to do?" the man replies good-naturedly. "I've got to pay bills. Con Ed, rent, diapers, I've got to make money any way I can."

"You selling crack?" Aliberti inquires.

"No, I don't sell crack," the man explains, scratching his head. "I'd rather do a robbery."

"So you have morals!" Aliberti chortles.

"No, it's not a question of morals," the man replies seriously. "I would never sell crack to a pregnant woman or to kids."

Aliberti doesn't answer, listening instead to the female voice of the police radio dispatcher as she calls out for a suspicious man, a possible burglar, lurking near a small lot adjacent to St. Cecilia's Church. Aliberti stomps on the gas pedal, leaving the toothless man to his own deeds, and speeds around the corner to 106th and Lexington Avenue. Turning off the headlights, he slowly eases the car to a stop at the front of the church. Grabbing their flashlights, he and Rivera gently close the car doors and lower their radios so as not to alert the possible burglar of their arrival.

"I almost forgot my hat," Rivera grimaces, returning to the car and placing his hat on his head at a rakish angle. If the Field Inspections Unit elected to scrutinize them, Rivera could be reprimanded for his missing hat and lose vacation days for not following police procedure.

Aliberti and Rivera shine their flashlights through the wire fence and over the brick walls of the church and the Julia De-Burgos Cultural Center. They look at each other and shake their heads. Rivera suggests driving to the other side of the building.

"Dude!" exclaims an exasperated Aliberti, attaching his red flashlight to his gunbelt, "He might be in there!"

With a short hop, he leaps onto the fence, his hands and feet sticking out like Spiderman in four different directions, in the diamond-shaped holes of the fence. He makes it over, and lands on the other side, adjusting his hat and pants and pulling out his flashlight again. Rivera, following police guidelines to stick with one's partner, has no choice but to follow. He curses. Although less agile and with larger feet, he grasps and kicks at the holes in the fence until he, too, pulls himself over. His hat miraculously stays in place.

The beams of their flashlights illuminate the walls, windows, and walkway of the two buildings. Nothing.

"If he was here, he isn't here now," surmises Aliberti.

Following the reverse method, they get back over and land unceremoniously next to their patrol car, startling an older black man walking his German shepherd.

Hispanic and black young men cluster in front of pay phones, playgrounds, and bodegas catering marijuana, heroin, cocaine and crack to customers from all over New York, New Jersey, and surrounding areas. Children as young as ten, called "Pee Wees," are recruited as lookouts. Ten dollars buys a tiny plastic bag filled with heroin.

Night after night during the summer, stifling heat becomes just an occupational hazard to both cops and criminals. Sometimes the night is eerily quiet with shadowy figures bobbing in and out of the Lexington Avenue subway, and a full moon hanging over the housing projects. Drug dealers and their lookouts—with the street names of MoMo, Click, Ajax, Ducky, James Brown, Lefty, Zulu, Smiley, Fats, Preacher—eye Officers Rivera and Aliberti. They all keep regular hours and sometimes order the same takeout. Aliberti and Rivera have worked together for almost a year, so they already recognize and know some of these young men and their trade. Nearly one-third of East Harlem's youth are unemployed; 26 percent of all arrests were of young men under the age of twenty-one. The average annual income of East Harlem residents is roughly $12,000; more than 40 percent are estimated to be on public assistance.

"How can most of them celebrate independence on the Fourth of July," questions Aliberti, "when they're tied to welfare?"

Yet parking spots are hard to come by. Lots in the housing projects are filled with old Toyotas and gleaming gold Lexuses; Aliberti once spotted a Porsche. "If people are so poor, how come everyone has a car?" he observes.

It was a typical midnight tour: A fourteen-year-old girl on Fifth Avenue is hit with bottles launched by two ten-year-olds. A nineteen-year-old white woman from 87th Street is standing on 98th and Third Avenue, and is suddenly smacked on the head with a stick by a Hispanic woman who demands, "Why you lookin' at my man?" A seventy-one-year-old woman insists that a fifty-five-year-old woman hit her on the head with a wooden cane in an argument over spilled garbage. A man is arrested for hitting his common-law wife with a mop handle. An eight-year-old is hit with a bat during an argument with a twenty-six-year-old man. A drunken man stabs a drinking buddy with a fork. A woman hits a male friend in the back of the head with a wooden statue. A mother hits her ten-year-old child with a tennis racket and a hot iron.

Young men, with nicknames like Big Red, Scarface, Chino, Fantasy, Speedy, Spice, Pop, Pancho, Ice, Chewie, Sweet Pea, Heavy, Pastor, and Sleepy, are out on the town and looking to transact and interact.

At twenty-six, with just two years as a police officer, Aliberti is edgier, more impatient and fidgety than his partner, and he wears an air of constant scorn. He prefers to drive so that he can dictate the pace for the evening. They pass a teenager urinating in the street. Aliberti presses hard on the brakes, backs the car up and stops. Perez and his partner pull up behind them. "You little fourteen-year-old piece of shit! You gotta change your ways."

Perez yells, "Hey, why don't you find a tree like the rest of the dogs in the neighborhood."

Their car speeds toward Third Avenue, where a young couple leans on a car, groping each other. Aliberti leans out the window and shouts, "Get a room!"

He drives with one hand on the wheel. Both the car radio and police radio are oddly silent, at least for the time being. Rivera fiddles with his watch as traffic slows to a stop on 96th Street. A panhandler with no legs moves painstakingly in his wheelchair down the middle of the road as he holds one hand out.

"Go somewhere else!" Aliberti calls out to the man, and turns their car onto 96th, heading west, and passes through a red light.

Larry Rivera's patience is wearing thin. "Marc, what the fuck is wrong with you?" he asks wearily.

Like a husband who has heard it all before, Aliberti replies, "Oh, Larryyy!" stretching out the last syllable until Rivera glares at him.

Aliberti speeds past city buses and livery cabs. "Slow down! *Slow down!* You must be writing your novel!" Rivera yells, eying the traffic. An illegal social club at 105th Street and Third Avenue lets out its underage and drunken customers, dozens of mostly black teenagers who stand idle on corners or wander through busy uptown traffic. They yell across the street at each other.

Rivera calls out, "No yelling in the street."

Aliberti adds wryly, "Good night, let's go. Clear the corner."

"You mean there's a law against yelling in the street?" one girl asks.

"People are trying to sleep," answers Rivera.

"But he's calling me."

"Go across the street then."

Aliberti drives slowly. "Hey, people are trying to sleep," he calls out. A group of young men don't budge. "Hey, guys. Don't move at your convenience," he says, edgily. "I asked—you—to move."

They walk away slowly.

The darkness is potentially violent; parties are ending or just beginning; arguments, too. An illegal gambling-numbers place had been raided and closed by police on 106th Street between First and Second Avenue the week before.

"People in the neighborhood were upset," Rivera says. "Someone made an arrest and the whole neighborhood came out. People were throwing glass and bricks. Glass was popping all over the street, coming from rooftops. If it hit a windshield, someone could have been seriously hurt."

"We basically have good people," Rivera explains as they stop for coffee at an all-night Korean deli. "The good, working people have to get up in the morning. We don't run into parents walking kids to school. We see the kids that parents obviously have no control over. Guns are more likely to be found on the four-to-twelve tour. But I think it's serious at any time. With the midnights, you're dealing with a lot more intoxicated people, and you have the drug trade.

"I used to work the day tour. It wasn't busy at all. There were very few guns. The people working the day tour are more of a family group. They pick their kids up and have the rest of the evening off. They're really not into making arrests. With the midnights, I've got more time to myself. I can eat dinner at home. I like the mentality of late tours. It's a smaller group and you don't deal with a lot of supervisors. There are conflicts but we still have to work together. The cops on midnights know what they have to do, what business they have to take care of. Work-wise, this is the tightest tour. People don't go to midnights to go out like they do on the four-to-twelve tour. That's the party tour and they all go out after work. Now, me, I really don't drink alcohol. To sit there with a bunch of guys talking to a bunch of guys talking about police work is not for me."

"Two-three, Boy," the dispatcher calls out.

Rivera keys the handset and acknowledges the call: "Boy."

"Missing child on East One Hundred Tenth Street." The female voice gives an address and an apartment and Rivera replies, "Four," short for an acknowledgement of 10–4.

On the second floor of a renovated, well-maintained building, Rivera, Aliberti, and two of their colleagues wait for Francisco Gonzalez to open his apartment door. To protect himself and his family, he has installed five locks and a chain on the door of his immaculate apartment. The door opens. He says that his twelve-year-old grandson is missing. It is 2:15 a.m.

"This isn't the first time," Gonzalez explains in lightly accented English. "He's uncontrollable. I'm raising my grandchildren. He likes the street. He picked one lock with a screwdriver and hammered off the other."

His wife stands quietly behind him in a flowered housedress. "What can I do?" Gonzalez asks, not really expecting an answer.

Rivera suggests that he take out a PINS warrant for his grandson. "PINS means 'person in need of supervision. You go down to family court, where you speak to a judge. With the PINS warrant, we can pick him up. In the meantime, if he's done this before, let's wait a couple of hours and see if he returns. Okay?"

The Gonzalezes agree and thank them, closing the door quietly.

The four cops walk to their cars just as a blockbuster goes off down the block. Two times the size of an M-80 firecracker, its power is equivalent to a quarter stick of dynamite. Aliberti and

Rivera instinctively turn toward the sound, then shrug, and get back in their car. They write notes of the evening's work in their leather memo books after Rivera speaks to the police dispatcher, advising her that the job has been handled.

They close their memo books. Aliberti tosses his on the back seat. The Arab owner of a bodega leaves his shop, followed by a young black man. As the two men approach the car, Aliberti orders them to stand back and gets out of the car.

"He comes in and breaks things," the owner complains. "He did this two weeks ago."

Rivera explains that he must call the police when it happens. The black man protests that he was being harassed. Aliberti looks at him strangely.

"Dude, if you don't like the service, why do you go there? Why give him your money?" he asks. "Go someplace else," he suggests, and turns to the bodega owner. "Why do you let him in here?"

The Arab and the black man look at each other and walk away, the owner back into his store, his customer in the opposite direction.

A Mexican man stumbles out of a bar so drunk that he walks into a wall. Aliberti shouts, "Viva, Mexico!" He adds, "But they get up and go to work in the morning. They're hard workers."

"Ten-thirteen. One-oh-nine and Madison Avenue. Anonymous caller," the dispatcher radios. A 10–13, the highest priority call, means a cop in trouble. It means every unit in the precinct responding with lights revolving and sirens screaming through the streets. When the call comes in from the dispatcher rather than the voice of a cop yelling for help, it isn't taken as seriously. But— just in case—every cop on patrol speeds to 109th and Madison, Aliberti and Rivera chase behind another patrol car.

"I have a Yodel in my mouth," Rivera says, swallowing quickly and gripping the dashboard. "You'll have to resuscitate me." When they arrive, the street is empty. "Central—ninety-X," Rivera groans, which means nothing to report. "People call in a thirteen for a number of reasons. Some get their thrills seeing us race by or there could be a big drug deal going down at the other end of the precinct and they want to get rid of us."

"Two-three, Boy. Family dispute," the radio crackles.

"**T**wenty-third Precinct, may I help you?" Officer Dwayne Rogers asks politely. "What's the address? I'll send the next car. Thank you. Have a nice evening," he says, hanging up the phone. He writes the address of a noise complaint—this time, a loud party—on a small piece of paper, which he gives to the next team leaving the stationhouse. Rogers, a bald black man with gentle eyes and quiet demeanor, works inside the stationhouse because of a leg injury. Earlier in the year, he and four other cops from the 23rd had responded to a call for a brawl going on outside a bar in the 19th Precinct. By the time they arrived, the fight had broken up. Rogers, standing outside the bar, was tackled by a drunken patron. "I don't know who the guy was," he said, sounding resigned. "He just blindsided me. Now I'm in pain and I need arthroscopic surgery. There's the possibility of being out for a year, a year and a half in rehab. I'm scared," he admits. "I never had an operation before. I'll never let it happen again. I'm not going to let people get close to me."

The stationhouse is quiet. Cells for housing prisoners are empty and there is no one waiting in the lobby to make a complaint. Aliberti points out his locker in the men's lockerroom in the basement. Large rows of metal lockers paired with wooden benches fill out the large space. Stickers with slogans decorate the lockers— "Proper Tactics Save Lives" and "Cover, Isolate, and Contain." Several rows of lockers also host taped-on *Playboy* centerfolds. The Police Department ordered them removed from every precinct after it deemed them offensive to women. Off to the right are the showers and bathrooms and in one stall, some creative cop has put circular *Oy!* stickers on the tiles. Like a high-school bathroom, the doors and walls of the stalls are scrawled with sayings. *Linda is a rat; No one likes Billy; Louise is a dyke.*

Down the hall in the musty basement is a smaller lockerroom filled with stale air, an old Christmas tree and a couple of beds where cops sleep if they have to stay overnight. Years ago, precinct lore has it, a man resided so far upstate that he lived in the precinct. His wife packed him off with frozen foods for a week. He ate and slept in the stationhouse, and went home on his days off.

Another Day in Paradise

Officers Edgar Cordero and Bob Kirby dub themselves, "Latino and Redneck." Kirby, squarely built with brown hair and wire-rimmed glasses, speaks in the same amiable terms to colleagues, complainers, and kids. He arrives promptly at the precinct every morning from his home on Rockland County, carrying a plastic container filled with the lunch his wife prepares. He has twelve years experience as a police officer, his partner, five. Cordero, born and raised in Manhattan, is more slightly built, with wavy black hair and a mustache, and an affectionate, easygoing manner. It is either too hot or too cold in their patrol car; they never seem able to regulate heat in winter or air conditioning in summer in their small office on wheels. While not maintaining law and order in East Harlem, the two partners, minus musical accompaniment, sing in hardy off-key baritones in their patrol car with the windows closed, their heads and hats bobbing to the beat of "Last Dance."

"Two-three, Eddie," the dispatcher calls, almost on cue as Kirby applauds Cordero's vocal performance.

"Eddie," a slightly out-of-breath Cordero responds.

"EDP, Second Avenue and One Hundred Sixth Street," she says—code for an emotionally distressed person—and gives an address in the Jefferson Houses, the public housing complex at the northern end of the precinct.

"There's a time to be loud and a time to go with the flow," says Cordero, pulling into a parking spot.

An elderly white woman, frail with tangled gray hair and lime-green polyester pants, opens the door of apartment 4F. "I'm going to kill myself and kill him, too!" a shrill female voice calls out, muffled from behind a bedroom door. They notice a refrigerator standing in the hallway and piles of clothing stacked precariously in corners as a roach falls from the ceiling onto Kirby's arm. Cordero brushes it off. A thin man in a polo shirt sits in a dirty, upholstered chair, his arms resting on a walker, in the small, crowded living room. "There's something wrong with her," he says angrily to Kirby and Cordero. "Oh, yeah, go ahead, do something!" he shouts to the woman behind the bedroom door.

Kirby and Cordero turn as she lets out a piercing yell.

"You bastard!" she shouts. "Go fuck yourself!"

"Miss, calm down. We're here to help you," Cordero says. "Just open the door."

"He's a bastard!" she shouts again. "Where's my slippers?"

"Your slippers are out here," Kirby says politely. "Come out and we'll give them to you."

"No! No! No!" she screams inconsolably.

"Take it easy," Cordero says calmly. "Just open the door."

Did she have a gun, a knife, a pot full of lye? Who would she attack first? Would she shout, pummel them with her fists, grab their guns? How would the media, the public, and the Police Department judge them if they had to shoot her? Was she another Eleanor Bumpers, the sixty-six-year-old emotionally disturbed woman who, after lunging at a cop with a butcher knife, was shot and killed in 1984? Adjusting their hats, they have their hands on their guns, just in case.

A large woman in a dirty flowered housedress, dingy white socks, and thinning hair yanks the door open. Kirby and Cordero flinch, their bodies tensing, their eyes focused on her hands.

"Excuse my language," the woman apologizes, an undercurrent of hysteria in her voice.

Cordero and Kirby relax; Cordero places his hand gently on her back. "Calm down. We're your friends," he assures her. "We're here to help."

"Where are my slippers!" she shouts, irate again. "Where are my slippers!"

"Goddamn retard!" the father spits out.

Cordero explains that a doctor at Metropolitan Hospital will be happy to see her but that he would have to put handcuffs on her wrists, both for her safety and for theirs. She holds her fat arms behind her and to spare her any embarrassment when they walk out of the building, Kirby folds a jacket over the cuffs so no one can see them.

Her mother finds her slippers; she walks into the elevator and out of the building in small, mincing steps, Cordero holding her by the elbow as if escorting her to the prom. She stumbles getting into the waiting ambulance as Cordero hangs on.

"I'm scared!" she shouts, shaking.

"That's okay. Take it easy, take it easy," Cordero says, soothingly.

The ambulance doors close and they follow it to Metropolitan Hospital. "We get more with sugar than with salt," Kirby says. "If you're looking for a fight, you'll get a fight. I want a peaceful day and then to go home."

"I joke around with everybody. I try and turn things around," Cordero says.

The woman steps out of the ambulance and begins to walk in the wrong direction.

"Where are you going?" asks Cordero, as if she should know better. "The dental clinic?"

The woman laughs wildly and begins crying as her mother takes her hand. "I'm so scared."

"Take it easy," Cordero says.

"I hate my father," she replies flatly.

As they enter the building, Cordero compliments her pedicure.

"I'm forty-five. He doesn't care about me," she says of her father, ignoring Cordero's remark. Kirby and Cordero accompany the woman to the psychiatric ward, where she is admitted for observation. As they return to their patrol car, a call comes in for a domestic dispute.

He is twenty-three, she is thirty, both black, both living in the same apartment. "He tryin' to get me to leave," she says angrily. "I ain't leaving." If she can prove she has lived in the apartment more than thirty days, then she as a legal right to be there, Kirby explains.

"My clothes are in the closets and in the dresser," she says. Her boyfriend sits silently on the edge of the couch, the zipper to his pants open. He plays a video game, ignoring the conversation. She flips through a messy pile of papers, looking for the one she needs. By the time she finds it, her anger has cooled. "Here, I have it," she declares, showing a bill with her name, address, and date from two months ago. Kirby says now it is a civil matter. "See? You can't get rid of me," she announces to her boyfriend. Kirby and Cordero close the apartment door behind them.

"Two-three, Eddie," the dispatcher calls out.

"Eddie," Cordero radios back.

"Drug dealing, male black, eighteen years old, Nike jacket, black baseball cap, East One Hundred Twelfth Street between First and Second."

"Four."

They circle the block twice, both heads turning to look into doorways and around corners, but they find no one fitting the description.

"Two-three, Eddie. X-ray," Cordero reports, giving the job back to the dispatcher.

Later in the day, Cordero and Kirby look downcast as they walk through the precinct toward the captain's office. They received a call for a suspicious man on a roof, they say, at a tenement building on East 112th Street, a crowded block with housing projects on one corner and smaller apartment buildings across the street. Young black and Hispanic men hustle drugs on the corners and benches, all with the same look: blue jeans, baggy shirts, and baseball caps. Cordero and Kirby had opened the front door of the tenement building and walked straight out through the back to look at the roof. Then they saw him: a Hispanic teenager sprawled on the pavement behind the building. He was dead. The boy's family blamed his death on Kirby and Cordero, insisting that they had pushed him off the roof. "We weren't even near the roof," Cordero says incredulously. Detectives investigating the case found eyewitnesses who confirmed their story, one asserting that the boy had been pushed by rival gang members. But the damage to Cordero and Kirby's morale was done, at least for the day.

"I see people being very arrogant and antagonistic to the police. They complain that they got a summons for double parking and want to know why they're being harassed. They're not being harassed. They got a summons. They're always looking to set up sides. They're positioning, like a line of scrimmage. People forget that someone called us here. We become the safety net for everything that's at fault," Kirby says. "It all comes down to one thing. People don't have enough respect for themselves. I care about people. That's the way I was brought up. There are still people out there entitled to and deserving of help, people who need help in spite of themselves. Some people have real psychological problems. A lot of people are coming here from third world nations, illegally or legally. They come from oppressive cultures where police were either a government operation or controlled by a paramilitary organization. Now all of a sudden, they've got rights, and with rights come responsibilities."

Cordero and Kirby get back into their patrol car, taking a few minutes to jot down the day's events in their memo books.

"I felt like a number when I started this morning," Kirby sighs, lifting his hat and smoothing back his hair.

"It's just a job," Cordero says. "I don't get affected by much anymore. Just babies and stuff. This is my job."

"At the end of the day, I forget what I did," Kirby says, turning the key in the ignition and steering out into traffic.

"Unless it's something out of the norm, like some crazy," his partner says. "Tomorrow is a brand-new day. It's not like you're here for the adventure. I have to be out here for sixteen more years. It depends on who you are. Some guys just don't have patience. You have to pace yourself, respond to emergencies. Don't kill yourself in the car, get there safely, maintain a level of composure and control. When you start losing sleep, it's time to shut down."

"In the beginning," Kirby says, "I used to dream about this job."

At a motorcycle repair shop, a man has come to pick up his motorcycle, demanding to pay by check. "Paying by check is against company policy," a mechanic says firmly. "My father's an attorney," his customer insists. "It's okay."

"Nowhere does it say you can give a check," the mechanic retorts.

"But he's got it all hooked up. It's ready to rock n' roll," pleads the owner of the motorcycle to Kirby.

"Look," Kirby says, "this man's not supposed to take a personal check. There's no I.D. Your father's an attorney. Talk to him about it."

"New Yorkers," he says when they're back in the car, "they're all like spoiled children."

They finally have a chance to eat at 2:30, an hour before they finish their day. Their last job is transporting a cop to Metropolitan Hospital to guard a prisoner. The cop, so skinny he is almost invisible, reeks of halitosis. He climbs in the backseat. "Man," exclaims Cordero, wincing, "your breath is kicking like Bruce Lee!"

They pass a sign for a candy store. "World of Nuts," notes Cordero wryly.

"Just another day in paradise," his partner sighs as they turn the corner.

One Size Fits All

Officer Steve Thompson isn't interested in camaraderie. "It's kind of foolish to fit in and try and be friends with guys who aren't your friends in the long run. I've strongly come to terms the last two or three years. That's why I don't really socialize. Everyone will sit around and they will talk about you behind your back. They're not really my friends. A lot of guys can't stand on their own. They have to stay in the crowd."

Before joining the midnight tour, Thompson worked both day and night shifts. "I couldn't stand getting up in the morning. I hated it. Four to twelve—I would end up drinking all the time.

Drinking, I was more or less trying to fit in with these guys. It was important to fit in."

Born in Harlem and raised in the South Bronx, Thompson is the son of a retired Housing cop. "When my father was on patrol, a lot of his buddies were boxing fans and half the precinct would be in my house watching a fight. I wanted to be part of his world. But . . ."

Thompson quietly dated a female officer on patrol, whom he later married. "It wasn't anybody's business. Guys knew we were going out and they would try and make her angry. They would make discourteous comments about her to see what I was going to say. It was difficult. It was extremely difficult. We were treated as outcasts."

His partner, Barry Travers, is also one of the dozen black cops in the precinct.

"It was kinda tough fitting in," Travers affirms. "We were the second or third group of minorities. There was a lot of resentment from the older whites, the Irish and Italian guys. A lot didn't want to talk to you or look at you. They had fifteen, twenty years on.

"It's fine now. There's a lot of young white guys who came on during the time we got on. Their attitudes are different from the older white guys, being around the same age. Their ways are different. There's a generation gap there.

"It's very hard to find cops who are individuals. Everyone wants to be like everyone else. People are afraid to be different. I guess they feel dependent, being a part of the group. They get to belong to something. One cop fires his gun, eight others do. Why? Because he did. But I can adapt to any environment, and Will's pretty much the same way."

A cop: "In East Harlem, if you talk to a cop, you're a snitch. '*Ese es una rata.*' This one's a rat. A lot of people don't want to talk to you because you're in uniform. If you talk to a Caucasian, it's community relations. If you talk to a black or Hispanic person, people are suspicious. We have a lot of young [cops] out there, not a lot of guys with street experience. The older people in this community say they're too young. 'What am I going to talk to him about? He's a child.' There's an age barrier. There are different little barriers within the community. They really don't know how to come across. 'What's this twenty-five-year-old going to do for me?' "

Officer Marc Aliberti: "I wasn't a well-liked person. I'm not an easy person to get along with. The way I hit the ground running, people didn't like it. I came on basically new and I put people to shame because I liked to work. I was giving out forty to fifty summonses a month. I was making the others look bad. The rumors followed me—that I was out of hand, a loose nut. The most important people in the precinct are [the one's] on patrol, and summonses are the big thing. If you write a lot of summonses—forty or fifty—are you a horse's ass? Cops, I guess, view it as a threat. I never viewed it like that. They treated me lousy. They put my locker in the bathroom. It sat there. Someone put shit on it. People put notes on it. They told me to slow down. It was a hint that I never took. It made me feel very low. I was devastated. I learned that people don't like to work and there's revenge if you step out of line."

Another cop describes a fellow officer: "He's a hairbag. He has thirty-two years as a cop. Thirty are his father's and two are his. I'm afraid of him. I don't like this guy. He has no manners. But there's nothing I can do about this. Otherwise, I look like a complainer and nobody will want to work with me."

Joe Barrato decided to add a hairweave to his pate for cosmetic reasons and, "Chia pet, to the desk," became his customary summons over the precinct loudspeaker. Diminutive, with large brown eyes and a beak nose, Barrato was a favorite target of precinct hijinks. According to precinct lore, he had been hung on a coathook by his gunbelt and tossed into a locker, which was then tossed into the shower. Cops say he never complained; that he had invited them over for barbecues and had been best man at another cop's wedding.

Tired of being the subject of crude cartoons and names, Barrato transferred and sued the Department for anti-gay harassment.

"We didn't know he was gay," insists a former colleague. "He wanted to be part of the group so badly that he never stopped anything."

Life, Liberty, and the
Pursuit of Shelter

Cops from the 23rd Precinct avoid the housing projects in East Harlem. "That's a Housing job," they sniff in derision as the police dispatcher calls out for Housing cops on the radio. But most of East Harlem is packed into cement boxes named after dead presidents and a dead peanut farmer. So when a call comes in for a suicide attempt in the Carver Houses, just across the street from Mount Sinai Hospital, three rookie cops on the way to their footposts reluctantly decide to respond.

"Aw, what the hell. Let's go," says Officer Steve Rosario, a short cop with a weightlifter's build and a crude sense of humor. The three amble over.

"Fuck the police!" calls out a teenager, sprawled on a bench. "We didn't call you."

"Well, somebody did," Rosario answers back, tipping his hat.

A short Hispanic man wearing a plaid workshirt meets them out front on Madison Avenue. "You the guy who called?" Rosario asks. The man nods. "It's my daughter," he says sadly.

The four men crowd into a metal elevator, the floors sticky from urine and grime. The man stands silently next to the control panel, staring at the floor. To them, he is nameless and even faceless. The three cops playfully poke at each other and laugh as they horse around.

"How old's your daughter?" asks Rosario.

"She's seventeen. She's having some problems with her boyfriend. She swallowed some pills."

Rosario pushes a tall, soft-looking black cop toward him. "Hey, we've got a guy for her!" he informs the man, who lifts his head. The parent speaks quietly and firmly:

"Fellas, this is not the time for this."

Unlocking the door to his apartment, the father leads them into his bedroom, where they find his daughter lying on a pillow, holding a teddy bear, her long black hair tucked underneath her arm. Curtains billow around a view of the courtyard below. Dressed in jeans and a T-shirt, she views them with interest. Her pit bull pup lets out a bark as they enter.

"So—whatya do?" Rosario asks casually, as if he were meeting a buddy.

"I swallowed my mother's AIDS medication," she answers, just as casually.

"Now, why'd ya do something like that?"

"My boyfriend broke up with me."

"A nice girl like you? You shouldn't be doing something like that," Rosario says and radios for an ambulance. The other two cops pet the dog, which jumps off the bed and runs in circles.

"Nice dog," says Rosario.

After the ambulance and its pair of paramedics takes the daughter and her father to the emergency room at Metropolitan Hospital, Rosario and his entourage stand on Madison Avenue, debating what to do for lunch. Officers in a patrol car pull up and join in the discussion.

"Fuckin' Housing," Rosario says. "They don't do shit."

Eleven housing developments means miles of cement-block hallways, monotonous brick facades, acres of grass, piles of garbage, and thousands of people. The only sign of distinctiveness is in the occasional garden tended by residents, and the graffiti that wallpapers stairwells and hallways. Otherwise, it's the same bleak monotonous buildings day after day: Taft, Jefferson, Johnson, Carver, Clinton, East River, MetroNorth and MetroNorth Rehab, Lexington, Wilson, White, and Washington.

Yet public housing is paradise for some. Older couples, or widows, raised families here and now live next door to young couples just starting out. Some consider it a step up from where they came from. Others can't wait to get out, and dream of living in better neighborhoods, and owning their own homes. There are retired elderly, women on welfare, employees of nearby Metropolitan Hospital, city workers and their families, and others. The playgrounds are filled with children during the summer, but when night falls, the drug dealers come out of the shadows. These young black and Hispanic men wait for their customers next to cement playground turtles, on benches, and in front of buildings. They work out of apartments, too. They move quickly, but an apartment filled with dealers can terrorize the hardworking residents of an entire building.

"It's not unusual to have three or four apartments dealing on one floor," says one Housing cop. "The rest are defenseless."

Housing Police handle all of the dilemmas of city life—and

then some. Routine police matters—murders, assaults, burglaries, robberies, rapes, and drug dealing—on public housing property are handled by Housing Police Service Area Five, which covers not only housing projects in the 23rd Precinct but those in the 28th, 24th, and the 20th. Since the merging of the New York City Police Department and the Housing Bureau in 1995, they have shared detective squads working out of the 23rd Precinct, and their arrests are processed through the desk sergeant there, too.

Housing is the police department of the poor and working class with a distinctive, relaxed, personal style. Precinct officers know their community intimately and completely. They walk incessantly around playgrounds, in and out of building lobbies, up and down stairs, and ride up and down in elevators. Housing cops handle bank drops once a month of rent checks, they report vandalism, the perpetual broken front doors, deal with people locked in and locked out of their apartments, dogs off their leashes, and mattresses in stairwells. They look for citable building conditions, reporting them to building management, and ensure that the maintenance office follows up. Every month they write down a list of areas covered with graffiti or signs and issue a report.

Housing cops listen to gunshots as they stand alone on rooftops. Domestic disputes are often handled alone. Cops do "verticals"— riding the elevator to the top of a building, and walking down through the stairwells, past graffiti and crack vials, keeping a wary eye out for people who have no business there. (Once, they found a sixty-nine-year-old white woman with cocaine.)

Many Housing cops know teenagers, criminals, and their mothers by name and occasionally find themselves summoned to their apartments during emergencies, like a flood from above when toilets and bathtubs overflow.

"Maintenance people need to get into the apartment," explains Housing Police Lieutenant Johnny Broderick. "They want the police to verify that nothing was taken. Housing concentrates more on little things. We're really into quality-of-life issues, very arrest oriented, more so than the Police Department. They seem to feel that we never pick up our jobs. We don't have enough people to cover. We're covering four different precincts and we have two different radio frequencies and three captains. Two-three cops try to have as little to do with us as possible. Housing people of higher rank are much more approachable than the NYPD. They eat lunch together."

Almost impossible to find without detailed directions, the East Harlem stationhouse of PSA 5 is located through a nondescript door to the left of the main entrance of the Taft Houses on Fifth Avenue. Cheap wooden paneling covers the walls. A roach crawls into a partially opened filing cabinet. The space is so small that lockerrooms for cops are located across the street in another building. The roaches are there, too.

"The basic difference right away is our facility. The Two-three is bigger, like a police house should be," explains Sergeant Lawrence Avery. "This is a disaster. They are building a brand-new PSA [stationhouse] on One Hundred Twenty-Fourth Street. We can't wait."

Manuel Vega takes out his white shirt and blue pants, the uniform of a captain, and prepares to dress in his tiny office for the four-to-twelve shift. Although he grew up in the South Bronx, housing projects are as foreign to him as to any cop from Long Island.

"In the early days, there were mostly gangs, the anti-police groups, the Black Liberation Army, the Hispanic groups," he says of the early seventies, when he was a rookie. "That was the beginning of the drug entry in the country. Drugs are our main concern. In my opinion, it's a profitable thing. It's hard to get rid of. It's a matter of dealing with symptoms. The dealers will leave. The people, from my point of view, are the victims. With drugs, there's an increase in weapons and access to weapons. That's been a major related problem. It's the symptom of the ghetto. It's used so openly. To see people living in this environment, at first it's shocking.

"It's peer pressure, or it's used in the house," he says about drugs. "When a cop sees someone affected by it, he develops a cushion so he's not personally affected. Anyone hypersensitive becomes too emotionally involved. Not that you don't want to show compassion—it's survival. The cops just want to help people and to provide resources, but it's frustrating sometimes. There are responsible, working people here. You have your criminal element, that's the exception.

"You don't have a way to recharge yourself. You develop a barrier. It's depressing to see what you have to see. This job has a way of consuming you. You just can't say, 'I can't do this tonight.'" Vega copes by jogging, reading books like *The Masculine Mystique*, and by practicing yoga. "I'd never tell anyone here," he says. "They wouldn't understand it."

At roll call, he reads off the list of cops, crowded shoulder to shoulder, his hands shaking from nervousness. Just as he did twenty years ago, most Housing cops still work alone.

Officer Paul Di Iorio opens an elevator door in the Jefferson Houses and removes a mattress that someone has deposited inside. "Now Housing cops go through stairs looking for debris because of fires," he says, adding, "even though it sounds more like a job for maintenance." He checks for mattresses in stairwells, too. In several buildings, these castoffs have been set on fire, igniting highly flammable paint on walls. In seconds, flames shot up the stairs, incinerating everything in their path, including a woman one time. "I never want to see this at Jefferson Houses," Di Iorio says. "There's no reason for any debris in a hallway. There are places for these things. People are lazy and don't give a shit. You risk your life and maybe someone else's."

He checks the motor rooms on rooftops for vagrants. Rooms are supposed to be locked, but locks are sometimes broken. One motor room is clean, the second sectioned off with a piece of plywood and used as a bathroom. Human feces decorate the floor in a corner.

"These buildings are attached," Di Iorio explains. "When you go from one to another to another, it's important to remember the address because they change from rooftop to rooftop, and if there is an emergency, you need to know where you are." In another motor room, he finds a sleeping bag and the remains of food; he will report it to management the next day.

Lobby doors are kicked in; locks are broken—a fulltime locksmith couldn't keep up with this problem. Tenants living in buildings feel threatened by people who don't belong there, who cluster in stairwells, dealing drugs, smoking or shooting up, or just hanging around. Di Iorio spots a congregation in one lobby at the Jefferson Houses. He doesn't need his key to open the door because the lock is broken again, a condition he adds to his report.

"What's your name, man?" he asks firmly, to one thin black man smoking a cigarette."

"Jack."

"Jack? Jack, where do you live?"

The man mumbles an address in the Bronx.

"Do me a favor. Take a walk down the block. Thank you."

"Where do you live?" Di Iorio asks the next person as he clears out the lobby.

"They can tell by your face what you're going to tell them," he says, holding the door open for an older black woman with a shopping bag.

"I stay in the house," she informs him. "Too many people out there getting killed."

Di Iorio walks toward a playground in the Jefferson Houses,

through paths of neatly tended grass, and up to a black teenager holding his hand in his pocket.

"What are you doing out here? What's up, man?" Di Iorio inquires. "What you got in your pocket?"

The teenager insolently pulls out a pen and aims it at the cop.

"I thought you were carrying a gun to protect yourself," Di Iorio says.

A black man passes by and whispers, "Second floor, man. Dealing crack, apartment twenty-six," and walks away. Di Iorio writes it down and walks through the light rain, drops sticking to his blue hat and blond mustache. He checks the locks around one door. They hold. A black woman with few teeth waits for him to finish, as a man comes up the walkway. Di Iorio knows him. "Man is a perp. Son is a perp," he says quietly.

Paul Di Iorio was born in 1957, the son of a Manhattan longshoreman from Naples, Italy, with a second-grade education. "We grew up at 501 West Twenty-eighth Street," he recalls. "My father believed that we should get the proper education. He worked his ass off. He busted his butt. He wanted us to be something. We grew up in the projects. Even if people didn't work, they had a great attitude. My father was very strict. I was an altar boy, too."

One of five brothers and sisters, the tragedy of drugs touched their working-class family, as well. "My sister Linda never finished high school. She was the oddball. She was the one with drugs, with the wrong guy. We tried to put her on the right track. She got her GED. She was on cocaine. She went to a program and was clean for six years.

"I never used reefer. I tried smoking cigarettes. I coughed the shit out of myself. That ended that. I used to drink rum and Coke with my friends. I went to the Catholic Youth Organization and they kept us out of trouble. They were very strict with us."

After graduating from high school in 1972, Di Iorio worked as a bank teller, handling new accounts. "I would have customers who'd wait just for me. You have to have the patience. I had the patience for the customers, and my supervisor appreciated it.

"My sister Florence was married to a cop. Steve worked in the Five-two in the Bronx. Every time he would come over, I'd see my mother and father. They'd treat him special. My mother looked up to him. She would roll out the red carpet for him. I said I wished that she did these things for me. I took the test in 1981 and I was called in 1983. I did it just so that my mother would do things like that. She was not paying any attention to me or to my brother. She had no idea of what I was going through.

"My God! What did I get myself into?" Di Iorio wonders. "The poverty level was so low. I never knew that any of these projects existed. I had no idea. If you would say something negative to someone, they would jump off at you. I learned not to fight but to reason, to talk. I have feelings for them. We all have feelings. You try and isolate yourself as a police officer. I am a human being. We're people, too. Things happen to us. They think that if you're a cop that nothing happens to you. We have a family life.

"I want to help," he says, sounding determined. "Child abuse is the worst. To deal with children who are abused, you want to kick the shit out of whoever did it. Sometimes it makes you want to cry. I've cried. I've gone to jobs where the kids are left completely alone. You see kids beaten with bruise marks.

"I feel for people who live here on welfare. I wasn't rich. I knew that I had to pick myself up to another level. I'd love to make more money. Who wouldn't? I've been here for thirteen years. I do not hate getting up and going to work."

Di Iorio narrowly misses getting hit by eggs lobbed from an apartment window. "It hasn't been a bed of roses for me," he continues, growing perturbed. "When people think that all people are the same, it burns me up. People come here and deserve to be in a safe environment. Drug dealers interrupt the business of life. There are no fathers here.

"A Spanish guy has been out here for a few days in a row," he says, pointing out a man standing in the shadows. "I'm sure he has a drug spot in the building. I see him here every night."

At the other end of the complex, a mother walks down the hallway of her building to throw her garbage down the chute in the compactor room. Her four-year-old accidentally closes the door behind her, locking her out. "He can't reach the knob," she says, sounding worried.

Di Iorio double-checks the locks and the door and calls for the Fire Department on his radio. "We used to have the master key for locked doors," he says. "The firemen have to break it down." He speaks into the door. "The fireman is here. Popi, we're opening up the door," he calls out to the little boy.

Three firemen arrive and take out one lock. The door still won't open. "Okay, we'll have to take out the other lock," one says. The door lock pops and mother and son are reunited.

The dispatcher radios for Di Iorio to respond to shots fired in an apartment two buildings over. He rushes over and stands next to the apartment, 4C, and rings the bell.

A black man answers the door, groggy with sleep.

"Do you know why we're here?" Di Iorio asks.

"No," he replies drowsily.

"Is everything okay? Do you know why we're here?"

"No."

"Did someone call from here?" Di Iorio asks.

"I don't know. My girlfriend just went out."

Di Iorio asks if he can come in and check. The man admits him. Satisfied that everything is okay, he apologizes to the man and leaves. It must have been a wrong address.

In the 1950s a tenant could be evicted from a public housing apartment for being a Communist. Today, dealing drugs isn't enough to warrant Di Iorio's intervening.

Although he may know who's selling drugs and what apartment

they live in, he cannot simply enter an apartment, arrest the drug dealer, and remove his stash, much less eject the dealers. Like 23rd Precinct cops, attacking these festering spots is up to narcotics units who set up their own investigations. Instead, Di Iorio can only move people from their perches in front of buildings and in playgrounds, arresting them only if he sees them dealing or using.

"With drugs—I feel that they have to get some help. That's a necessity," he insists. "If I see them sleeping or derelict or smoking reefer, technically it's my discretion. I don't always lock them up. I try and educate them. Why not educate them? I refer them to an agency. Sometimes I'll get the info for them and call myself, especially mothers who are on drugs and who have children. You give the information to people and hope that they will take it. You have to work with management and with the community or things will go crazy."

Di Iorio, because of his skills and seniority, holds the rank of detective specialist. "I prefer staying on patrol. I was asked to consider going into the Detective Bureau. I said no. I've spent so many years on the street. I don't want to lock myself in an office," he says, walking along a pathway to another building. "I like being out here. We are more community oriented, I feel, than the Two-three. We were trained toward helping the people. I'm here to serve the community and do it the right way. If you are a positive figure, you will see positive results. You're visible. The most important aspect of your job is that you're visible. People are looking out. They know that they have a cop out there. You can't go to your post and hide. They live here. You don't."

Di Iorio recalls walking toward a robbery suspect in the lobby of a building. "I came out with my gun. I told him, 'Freeze! Put your hands up in the air.' I was a split second from firing. There's the tension of blacks being shot by white cops. That was in the back of my mind. My adrenaline was pumped up. I looked at his hands. He didn't have a gun. He said, 'Officer, don't shoot.' He threw the gun out from his waist and took off and ran. I jumped on him and cuffed him. It was a good arrest. Five years later I'm sitting in a patrol car. The guy says, 'Officer Di Iorio. I'm the one you locked up in that robbery.' He said, 'Man, I want to thank you. I've changed my life. I'm going to go straight.' It was a positive end. There we were, five or six years later, and he recognized me."

He recalls a woman who was been beaten up by her boyfriend so badly that her jaw was broken. Di Iorio had spotted the boyfriend later that day. "I said, 'Yo, man. Come over here. I want to talk to you.' He was going to run. I got him in front of his building. I grabbed him and he slipped. I knew where he was going. He's going through his pockets. He got out the gun. I said, 'Freeze! Let me see your hands.' His dogs turned on me. I took two steps back. I thought they were going to chew me alive. I shot six times, he shot four and he got away. I was scared. The fear alone scared the hell out of me," Di Iorio says. "The shooting took fifteen seconds, the investigation six hours.

"I don't know how to define the scaredness," he says. "It makes you paranoid. You just don't know how to react. It happened so fast—in seconds, five to seven seconds. My first year, I woke up strangling my wife. I had her in a headlock. I dreamt that I was involved in a shootout. I was going after one guy. I was fighting him. She had to punch me to wake me up. She worries every day."

At the monthly meetings of the Jefferson Houses Tenants Association Meeting, Di Iorio and building managers meet with tenants. The tenants complain about apartment and building repairs while the Tenant Patrol complains that they haven't seen enough cops. Others complain about broken front doors to their apartment buildings.

"We're planning on putting in doors that swing around to the outside so they can't kick it in," the manager said. "We always try, try, try. We feel bad. The children—that's our future. The old people, the poor people feel trapped. We try to make it as pleasant as we can. There are so many negative forces against us. It's frustrating. We remove graffiti on an ongoing basis. You can't let up for one day."

A resident, an older black woman, with two dogs in a stroller and bows in her hair, gives a testimonial: "People call it El Barrio. Some people say it's a ghetto. I never heard of the word *poverty* or *ghetto*. I don't get caught up with that. I see nothing wrong with these strong buildings. We've had nice, nice times here. Gunshots? I haven't heard a gunshot in a year. They need to get everyone out of here who's dealing drugs. It's almost something you can sense. They should be in school or in college. They shouldn't be hanging out all the time. My son has seen too many of his friends dead. He'll go on with his life. Selling drugs, that's stupidity."

Di Iorio stands up to give his report from the table in the front of the room. "These are all the arrests that took place during the month. Thirty-eight. I made about fifteen. We're coming into the Twenty-third Precinct every three days with an arrest. Eighteen misdemeanors, crack vials," he reads from his report, "six felony arrests for sale of narcotics, twenty-four arrests in narcotics, nine arrests criminal trespass, one hundred ninety-one summonses for narcotics and drugs, fifty-three parking summonses, two disorderly conduct, and eight ECBs. These are summons from the Environmental Control Board for drinking of beer and animals off the leash." Before he can finish, the tenants give him a round of applause.

"We're instructed to arrest people urinating in public. We had one arrest, criminal possession of weapon," he continues. "One knife, one robbery. Last month we had eleven so there's been a decrease of ten. We've had an impact in the last month. You guys have seven officers here in Jefferson Projects every day at one time."

A woman complains of a neighbor's son who was convicted of rape. "There's a known rapist riding in and out of the elevator," she says. "My neighbor in 3A is afraid to ride the elevator."

"If I ever see him, you won't have to worry about him anymore," Di Iorio assures her.

"Even so," says an older black woman, "I refuse to move. This is a beautiful area."

"Most of us are stuck here," says artist and social worker Juan Andujar. "People don't have the means to live elsewhere. They're subjected to living in East Harlem. Where are they going to move? The working person doesn't make that much. The only way to make it are drug deals, or you hit the Lotto. When you don't make that much, what do you do? You have people, traditionally the poor, on welfare. It's hard to get out of the neighborhood."

Di Iorio stops back at the PSA 5 stationhouse to pick up his dinner, passing by a plaque dedicated to Officer Shawn Dunston who was shot and killed in the line of duty in 1982. Di Iorio greets Officer Artie Bowles, who, at fifty-two, is thirty years older than some of the cops he works with. A veteran of the Vietnam War, Haus has worked as a Housing cop since 1973. He worked with Dunston.

"Three or four perps had information that this one man had a lot of money," Bowles remembers. "He didn't believe in banks. He did his banking in his apartment. The family members were there, with the exception of the father. The perps found their way in. They herded them all in one room. They missed a young girl between five and ten. She called the Housing Police seven-digit number. She was interrupted when one perp discovered her. They were aware of the fact that she called. Dunston and his partner responded. They were in the Washington Houses, Two-fifteen, East One Hundred Second Street. They responded, they knocked on the door.

"One perp answered the door and opened it. Dunston and his partner could see the family in the living room. One of the perps did all of the talking and then Dunston saw something in the expression of the people. He took a step in. There was a perp behind the door with a shotgun when he entered. He shot Dunston in the neck. His partner fired back. They exchanged fire. The partner backed down. He was firing with a thirty-eight. He wounded one of the perps. He called for help.

"The first car that responded retrieved Dunston, who was still alive, and brought him down in their car. They took him to Met Hospital. He lost a lot of blood. The bullet entered his neck at close range and exited behind his ear. He lost too much blood. The doctors did try. They opened up his chest and manually massaged his heart. It was too late. He didn't make it. He had just made his tenth anniversary—the halfway mark—the same week that he died.

"It had to be around four p.m. We all ran out. We interrupted roll call. We thought maybe we'd give some blood and then shoot over to the hospital. By the time that we got there, it was no use. It was over. I was in shock. I couldn't believe it. I can still feel that feeling," he says, turning away quietly.

"I accompanied the body to the funeral home. That was when it hit me. I was saddened in the church. One of the guys read the eulogy and he was so overcome with emotion he couldn't finish. Dunston and seven of us were in the National Guard together. We were in the same company. We had our monthly drills. We saw each other a little bit more than on the job. I was touched at the chance to have known him.

"I listened to Taps over the open grave. The casket went in. All you have are memories. He was very outgoing, wise. When he walked into a room, you'd hear it. He and his wife were in the process of buying a house. He was upbeat about that. He had twin girls.

"I think about him. I never saw his wife and kids again. His partner didn't work here for six to eight months. They sent him to another command. He was limited duty. They wouldn't let him go out on patrol. He had problems. He would break down and start crying. He came back and then he worked nine or ten years. We were worried about him. He was thinking if he had taken one little step or half step, he wouldn't be here today. That little half step. There are lessons to learn.

"I don't think that it changed me that much. Maybe the sense that we can all go at anytime," he says, as the telephone rings, "that it happens so suddenly."

"*H*ousing 131." Central calls Di Iorio over the radio. *"Possible drug overdose."*

Di Iorio walks quickly through another nondescript building in the Jefferson Houses. The apartment door is open. A chubby Hispanic man, with a few extra chins, sits on his flowered couch, his eyes barely open, his arms and legs spread out. Paramedics have already arrived.

"Are you allergic to any medication?" one asks.

"Ricardo! Are you allergic to anything?" he asks again, a little louder, slapping his arm.

Ricardo opens his eyes and mumbles, "Tomatoes."

"Well," says Di Iorio, "we're not going out for pizza."

Samuel, eighteen, says that he first had sex when he was six years old. "That was with my godsister. I didn't know what I was doing," he says. "She was five. You didn't know about sex. We were always humping. We thought cabbage made you pregnant." He sits on a bench next to his girlfriend, sixteen-year-old Shanice.

"I didn't mean to get pregnant," she says. "I don't believe in abortion. I didn't even know about protection. I wasn't surprised. If you don't use protection, you know something's going to happen.

My mother? I don't have no idea where she is. I think she's in Virginia. She's been arrested for everything. She was arrested for hustling and she got into trouble three times this summer. I haven't been living with her since I was six. My father died of cardiac arrest when I was eleven. He didn't have no occupation. He did little jobs. I was sure he was in drugs."

Samuels refuses to give up smoking blunts—marijuana-laced cigars—and drinking forty-ounce bottles of beer. Shanice refuses to give up junk food.

"I eat regular stuff," she says, patting her small belly and eating a package of chocolate doughnuts. "I be craving stuff that I like. I eat what everyone else eats. I eat McDonald's and at that fried chicken place. I want my baby to grow up good. I want to work either in a clothing store or in a hospital. I don't want to work in a fast food store. Public assistance—I don't want to do that. That ain't no way to teach your child to be. You teach your child to work. I always did for myself. They say you're going to live happily ever after," she says, tossing the plastic doughnut wrapper on the ground. "They don't tell about problems, about the real world. Life is not a fairy tale."

Although their four children have moved out, Iris and Jose Hernandez still live in their airy apartment in Franklin Plaza. The complex has been described as an oasis in the middle of East Harlem, stretching from 106th to 108th Street between Third and First Avenues. Many of its tenants are middle-class blacks and Hispanics residing there for over twenty years, raising families in low-income co-ops. An active tenants' association and an organized management group work closely together, and the immaculately kept grounds boast vegetable and flower gardens, tended by residents. Picnic tables, a basketball court, a room for senior citizens, and a nursery school dot the complex, while a private security force patrols the grounds. Residents of Franklin Plaza gather to stroll and sing Christmas carols during the holiday season.

The Hernandezes' son, Louis, remembers the lure of gangs in East Harlem during the sixties. "Second Avenue was more guinea turf—Italian. It meant crossing that boundary was dangerous. Here, I lived between two blocks of Hispanic gangs. I didn't fit in either, so I would get my ass kicked between either the Turbans or the Dragons. I was bigger physically than other kids my age. You either become a bully or get bullied on. Later on, I didn't join gangs because they started to disappear. Gangs began to dwindle because of drugs and guys going to Vietnam. Vietnam was also an introduction to drug culture. But you couldn't be fighting and nodding out at the same time. And here, there was a division between the heavy narcotics scene, the drinkers, and the peace-and-love hippie types. Everyone took pot and mescaline." Hernandez, too, experimented with drugs as a teenager. "I used to go to the Latin Quarter [a nightclub]. I used to walk into the bathroom and see O.D.s in there. I would try and revive my friends.

"I started off with booze and then I was introduced to marijuana. I was shy, introverted, insecure. And then I was introduced to pills. I avoided heroin.

"I hung out with some bad apples. We would harass whites and create havoc. I was under the impression that they had wronged us. I was only going with what was fed to me. It was a sense of entitlement. It was odd. It seemed like we were fronting. It was a front, always fronting, carrying this image. And it was this fear of being in a place alone."

Louis Hernandez, forty-four, looks up to his stepfather, Jose, a dignified man with white hair and warm but serious brown eyes. "He came into my life when I was eight years old. Jose was the first real male image who seemed to be permanent. He worked a lot of hours in a hotel. He was always very formal and very clean cut. He wasn't abusive. He was very responsible financially. My mother was also very strict. There was structure and discipline. Jose exemplified someone who works. He wasn't a man who was formally educated. I used to correct his English. He always felt that he didn't speak well. He wanted us to go to school. But I've met kids who haven't grown up with a father who grew up very well. Others with fathers, they're dead."

Louis's mother, Iris, remembers her son's friends. "When you live in a neighborhood like this, you worry. A lot of Louis's friends had died. One friend, he was very bright. He was studying to be a doctor. He died from an overdose. He was going to City College. Very few made it. I really don't understand how it happened. Since I was working at a community center, I knew a new drug when it came out, what to do, what to look for. I was always checking.

"We used to have family meetings in the living room, my husband and I. What bothers you? The telephone calls and how many you're entitled to. Why are you mad at your sister? Why are you mad at your brother? They used to open up. That's why we managed. When they had a boyfriend, I want you to bring him upstairs. I used to have them sit down, give them a sandwich and coffee. Where do you live? Who are your parents? Do you go to school? The kids were so embarrassed."

Louis Hernandez has been a public school teacher since 1977, earned a second master's degree in guidance counseling, and a postgraduate degree in family counseling. "You have to teach the kids out there survival skills, to develop some type of judgment skills, to have some kind of career," he says. "We're getting more crack babies and foster situations. Family structures have been altered dramatically. It's easy to have sex, but not easy to stick around for the results. It's expected that women can be raped by a certain age. 'Don't you know you have rights?' " he asks his students.

He sits in his office in a junior high school on East 109th Street. Students wander in and out.

"It brings a certain emotion to the pit of my stomach, as the protector. Drugs, violence—people are killing each other. You always have that group—if they make it, they want to get the fuck out of here. If you don't feel motivated, then you stay where you're at.

"I was afraid to leave, too. I had all these excuses," he says.

"They're afraid to leave the neighborhood. There are very few who even leave to go to camp or to Great Adventure [Amusement Park]. Somewhere, love—trust—was violated. In the beginning that's one of the basic stages of life. Trust is a major issue. It's cyclical, 'You treat me like shit. I'm going to treat you like shit.' It just keeps on going. You perceive this as rejection and you're stuck. You want the best for them and you want to send the message that education is the best thing you can do for yourself. But there are a lot of success stories. Kids go on to Cornell, Yale, Harvard."

Hernandez's younger sister, Andrea, an assistant principal, teaches bilingual education at a grade school across the street from where her brother works. "You see the sickness in the community. It's important to focus on the beautiful," she says, from her small, crowded, colorful office. "You have to focus on the good in the community. You have to re-create this place. I do it with the kids. When I see them learning, that's what it's all about."

While Under the Influence

One cop says about 35 percent of the cops at the 23rd drink. "Drinking is part of our culture," says Captain Matt Carmody. "As a cop, you have to be in control. There's this culture. Drink and drugs are all self-medication. I've seen less drinking on tours than fifteen years ago. People then were the hard-core drinkers. The job might have been a contributing factor. Very few people who are with the job become alcoholics. They have emotional problems and they might start to do it more. So it's everywhere."

Officer Walter James estimates that ten to fifteen officers of the two hundred in the precinct are heavy drinkers. "But no one admits to it. Our stats are no higher than any other industry. We're just like any other drunks. There are drunks on the stock market or any other job. I think a small percentage drink because of the stress, just like any other industry that drowns their sorrows. And for a new cop, that's the way it is. I continue to do it for social reasons. I've worked with a lot of guys who don't drink. It's just part of the socializing process. Seventy-five percent will go out and have a beer now and then over the course of six months. Every platoon has their clique that goes out. In the Two-three, sixty percent of people go out. It's easy to get caught up in the whole thing. You're drinking out of a pitcher, talking and bullshitting."

"I think it's stupid," scoffs Officer Tara Casey. "It comes with your identity and wanting to relate to the boys. You want to prove yourself by drinking and hanging out. A lot of marriages are going to be in disarray because these guys are always hanging out. You might find females but it's not the norm. There were certain women that go out for a beer. They want to be a part of the crowd. Me? I don't give a shit."

One cop often has alcohol on his breath when he arrives in the morning. Another, neighborhood residents say, stands in a bodega in the precinct, drinking a beer while in uniform. A third could be found in front of a corner bodega after his tour had ended, a bottle of beer in his hand. After several stints in alcohol rehab, cops said his drug test came back positive and he was finally fired. Thirty-five cops in the New York City Police Department failed drug tests in 1998, down from forty-three; more than half of the drug test failures were from cocaine.

Captain Carmody, a recovering alcoholic, refers cops he suspects of having a drinking problem to Alcoholics Anonymous. "People always get the Bowery Bum impression and that doesn't really happen. Most are workaholics. They're good workers when they're not drinking. They're intelligent, sensitive, attentive to detail. People my rank and above don't go around telling me, 'Yeah, I'm an alcoholic,' " he says wryly. "The Police Department will take your guns instead of trying to see if they can help you. It was always drilled into my head—'You'll get fucked. It'll go onto your record.' How can I turn around and say that I never drank? There are people ranks above me who don't drink anymore. They couldn't. Their heads are in the sand." He laughs. "They are too high and mighty to admit that they have a problem. Start because of the job? I doubt it. It's easier to say. I started drinking when I was eleven. In high school I was drinking a whole bottle of whiskey like a fuckin' maniac. I went into the Marine Corps, drank crazily there. I didn't drink much at home. There was drinking in the radio car. I drove around and drank. I'd meet the other guys and drink."

Early in his career, Captain Carmody once left the precinct with his patrol car. "I took the car and a blond waitress down to the Jersey Shore. Everyone knew I was a drunk. My life was unmanageable. You don't make phone calls on [other cops]. It's testament. You don't drop a dime. They don't drop a dime on someone committing a crime. It's a military culture. You can't turn around and say we need help. It's a sign of weakness. It's admitting that your life is controlled.

"A beer today would be perfect," he sighs. "I know guys who have had fathers die of alcoholism and they're the biggest fuckin' drunks I know. People get suspended for being drunk on duty. It's real easy to run away from your problems. At PBA meetings, all everybody did was stand at the bar and drink. It's coming from the culture."

Cops drinking while driving usually don't have much to worry about. Cops, as a professional courtesy, will not issue a summons to another cop. A cop, pulled over for a traffic violation or for drinking while driving, flashes his badge and off he goes. His record is clean. One 23rd Precinct sergeant was pulled over by cops in Nassau County for drunk driving more than once; a not-too-discreet telephone call was made to the Police Department and he was shipped to alcohol rehab for his protection and others.

"Cops are not going to get stopped because they're the police," Captain Carmody confirms. "Except if they're in Nassau County, where they're trying to protect citizens from getting run over by a drunk cop."

Cops complain that they're not perceived as people as they face many of the same issues and pressures as others not in their world—paying bills, child support, divorce, car loans, depression, illness, stress, and burnout. Many fear that if these problems were exposed to their peers and the public, they would be stigmatized in such a macho culture.

If they choose to, cops may come forth and seek help anonymously through different Department-sponsored programs; others are forced to by the PBA. One cop says, "If they know someone is going to get jammed up, the first thing the PBA says is, 'Go to the farm.' The PBA will run someone in. If you don't go to counseling unit, you won't make overtime. They'll take your guns."

"Cops are sent to the farm to cover up drug use but," the captain says angrily, "possession of drugs is a crime. How can the Department acknowledge this? It's a place for cops and firemen to go anonymously. It's [a double standard] condoned by the Department as a way of helping them. I don't understand it. The PBA's job is to protect him and get him to the farm. It's accepted if you go. You're granted amnesty. It's nothing new. People show up for duty who haven't gone home yet from the night before. Being a junkie is not a crime. But a junkie cop is like you're admitting to committing a crime. You're sworn to uphold the law. It puts you in a separate category. You're held to a higher standard. Seeking help is a way of getting you out of something. It's a cosmetic cover-up."

Taking away a cop's shield and a gun may be traumatic, and

the threat is used against them. If an allegation is made against a cop for domestic abuse, his or her guns are removed as a precautionary measure. "I had a domestic thing. You're not supposed to be human," says one male cop. "They take your guns and shield, and it takes months to investigate."

One cop says that he thought another might be suicidal: "He mentioned that he was considering ending his own life," the cop says. "He only mentioned it once. I don't know him that well. What if I'm wrong? Now he gets his guns taken away and it goes on his record."

Protected like other jobs by a union, it's almost impossible to fire someone for incompetency. Cops get transferred instead, and one precinct's problem cops become another's. There is a network of cops at every precinct who never leave. When an officer transfers from another precinct, or when a precinct gets a new commanding officer, a reputation—real or unfounded—may follow.

"One or two people make a call or send a fax. The stories were very bad and that got around," one cop says of a fellow officer. "They would look at you and say, 'Why is this guy here?' If you're a fuck-up, there'll be phone calls. On this job, a lot of people don't like the attitude of others. They're getting away with murder while other guys are really working. 'I should be getting what you're getting.' If you're transferred, you're either a screw-up or nothing. Why would you want to leave? You become comfortable. Everyone knows who you are."

I was going to John Jay. I said, 'Mom, I'm going to be a cop.'" Luis Cepeda recalls. "She said, 'If you become a cop, you can forget that I'm your mother.' The family was getting worse and worse. Satanic powers took them over. When I was a big dealer, they wanted to be big dealers, too. We had to deal with the witchcraft in every room. They don't like to talk about these things. Ana violated her parole. It was drug related. She came out positive for HIV. Cheo, he gets thrown in jail for being drunk and fighting. Almost everyone in the family is on public assistance. You went the way you went," he says, shrugging his shoulders.

"At the end of the sixties, that's when I lost control. A father would have made a difference. Today, it's very hard to bring up kids without a father. The presence of the father is very important if he's strong. They look at the father as a role model.

"We used to rule this area," he says, looking across the street at the baseball fields. "Ninety percent of people we knew are dead. Ten percent are kind of downhill. I used to know everybody on One Hundredth Street. It wasn't peaceful when you're on the top. People dare to take chances with you. Nobody took a chance with me because they wouldn't last too long. Nobody knew where I lived or where I came from. I never stayed in one place too long. I had four different apartments to sleep in. I was a playboy. I had one apartment where the girls paid the rent, the girls were working. I didn't go out with women who wanted to take money out of me. I didn't buy a car when I was in the City. I didn't want no one to follow me. I called a cab. The taxi knew what I was doing. I gave a hundred dollars a week for a drive. They used to drop me off. I used to have a sawed-off shotgun in the house, a forty-five over the door, a Magnum three-fifty-seven on the door. I also had a little five-shot thirty-eight. I used it to shoot at the air. I had a hand grenade, a whiz gun—a machine gun that fired forty-five [caliber] bullets. We had an Uzi. We used to get everything. Like in the movies, everyone had big weapons."

Cepeda's daughter is twenty-six, his son a year older. "My son wanted to be a cop, too," he says. "But he was in the wrong place at the wrong time. He was busted for coke. He was in his mother's house. He was doing good at John Jay. It was very disappointing. It came as a shock to me. If we had money and a good lawyer, he wouldn't have had to do time."

Cepeda found God at the Church of the Revelation in the Bronx, where he now lives with his second wife, Marta. "Back in 1990, I noticed something changing in me. I started preaching to people," he says. "This light came from behind a tree. It got bigger and bigger. All my hair stood up. My wife said, 'God is calling.' I cried for half an hour. I could not stop crying. I went to a retreat. I asked Him to restore all the damage that I did. The Bible said, 'When you go to Jesus you become a new man.' The only thing I miss is the money. Now the police recognize me as a clergy. The police know the people in the neighborhood. I see a new batch, they really do care. They're young. They see the abuse of others. They stopped me a couple of times. They don't curse at me. Police officers, they know we pray for them."

Guns and Noses

New Year's Eve, Officer Leo Pappas and his partner, Ivan Moreno, split up to get back into their patrol car. But the doors won't open. "Uh-oh, I think we're locked out," says Pappas. It was just a few minutes before midnight and he looks around nervously at darkened windows and rooftops. "All we need is someone to start shooting," he mutters as he radios another car to come around with a slim jim. "We're sitting ducks out here."

With just a minute to go before the ball in Times Square drops to mark the start of the New Year, he pops the door open and the two partners scramble in and take off. "This is the place where everyone tests out their Christmas presents by heading to the roofs of their buildings and shooting off their Tech-nines into the night air. The safest place is in the tunnel," Pappas advises.

The tunnels—Amtrak railroad underpasses—split the neighborhood and separate housing projects from tenement houses. Each patrol car has its own opening underneath the tunnel. "We're not using sirens—no use in getting attention—they'll shoot at us," Pappas explains. They speak of a man on the stairs with a rifle. "I don't know what he had. Maybe it was a howitzer. Good thing he didn't open up," Moreno says. "Ten-nine-eight-seven-six-five-four-(shut the radio off at one)-three, two, one! Happy New Year!" yells Dick Clark, as he does every year. And every year in East Harlem, the yell is echoed back with gunshots.

Gunshots come from somewhere behind the car, from rooftops, shots across Park Avenue as a train rumbles overhead, accompanied by noisemakers and explosions of firecrackers. "They traded in old guns, got money, and used it toward newer ones," says Moreno. "These are all guys who got guns for Christmas."

"Does sound like Sarajevo, doesn't it?" asks Pappas, leaning back in the seat. "I've been here for New Year's for nine years and I haven't been shot yet," adds his partner.

Someone squawks into the police radio, *"Scrooge! Happy New Year!"* An angry voice shouts, *"Get off the air! Don't be a rookie! People are working out here!"*

"I think there are a lot of good people in this neighborhood," says Moreno.

"All the good people are in the house now. All you see is all the shit out here," Pappas says.

They move out of the tunnel as the rain begins, drops pinging off the roof, and the gunshots subside. "They don't want to get their new Tech-nines wet," scoffs Pappas.

There is no shortage of guns in East Harlem. The 23rd Precinct's anti-crime unit focuses on guns and stolen cars, working in un-

marked cars and in plainclothes. They bring in the more signifi-
cant weapons and ammunition. The unit is informally headed by
Officer Alan Patrick, the son of professional musicians, whose
girth strains car seats and shocks but who partners with a light,
fleet-footed cop who can outrun anybody.

"Alan can look at one hundred people and pick out a guy with
a gun," says a cop. "He's white trash, but he knows what he's
doing."

"The more people you stop, the more guns you find," says another cop flatly.

"He's not interested in whether it's legal or not. It's a numbers game. The more you stop, the more you'll find," repeats a
third.

"I can't stand what he does, but what am I supposed to do
about it?" another cop protests. "The Department wants the numbers, the public wants to feel safe, we get the guns, he does what
he wants."

A cop says, anonymously, "You want guns, guns, guns—you
toss everybody in the street. I could go out and toss everybody. Is
that legal? If you have a bulge, I can go feel for it just because I
need an arrest. There are millions of guns out there. Nobody's
going to go, 'Look, I have a bulge.' Never in a million years are
you going to see a gun protruding. Everyone says the same thing.
'I saw a silver object.' Never in a million years can you see it. To
me, that's perjury. I don't want to lose my job. They're going to
keep tossing until they come up with someone. One day they'll
get stuck with a lawyer who'll sue the shit out of their pants. They
wouldn't toss a white person in a million years. You have to look
mighty suspicious. You see a black or Hispanic person in the
Nineteenth or Seventeenth [precincts], he must be looking to rob.
White people are up here to get drugs, buying a hit. People get
robbed here all the time."

One officer reported to Internal Affairs the illegal stops and searches for guns by his colleague and his failure to fill out stop-and-frisk reports.

"Nothing happened. This guy is a fuckin' liar," the officer says. "The assistant district attorneys know that [the accused cop] can't be trusted. But he always seems to get away with this."

A team of three Anti-crime cops turns off a football game and leaves their office carrying a stack of stop-and-frisk reports which they are required to fill out. This evening, Alan Patrick and two cops, both Puerto Rican, cruise the streets in a gray, hard-to-mistake undercover car, wearing street clothes and chains with their police shields. On their wrists are orange sweatbands, the color of the day that will distinguish them as police officers. Patrick drives; their police radios are turned up. "We're the cowboys of the precinct," Patrick explains. Both Puerto Rican cops begin singing Glen Campbell's, "Rhinestone Cowboy."

Passing a teenager toting a large bookbag, Officer Richie Vega acknowledges, "It's a tough place to bring up a kid. They have to learn the streets. You see something, step away. I was born at Met Hospital, I turned out to be fine. It depends on your upbringing. There's a lot to stay away from. I never came out at night, to avoid things."

A man reaching into his waistband causes alarms for many cops. "But that doesn't necessarily constitute a stop," explains one sergeant. "We have to wait until he does something."

"What?" says another cop. "Shoot one of us?"

Their unmarked car slowly turns the corner, and Alan Patrick eyes a black man crossing the street.

"Hey, man! Why you stoppin' me?" the black man cries out under the glare of the headlights.

"Because," says the fat cop as he beckons him over, "you're black."

The black man looks at him quizzically. The cop winks. They

both laugh. The cop pulls off, onto 102nd Street, and parks in front of the 23rd Precinct.

Back out again, Patrick drives slowly across 112th Street—"Hey, look! No brakes!" he demonstrates. A tall, thin, black teenager walks toward the car, looking nervously at the car and away again, his right arm in an awkward position, as if he were holding something in his waistband. To Patrick, this means one thing. "Oy, vey," whispers Officer Vega.

Patrick stops the car. "Hey, guy! Where are you off to?" Vega asks, jumping out of the car. He pounces on the suspect, and he and his partner push the teenager face down onto the hood. Vega runs his hands along the suspect's body. "Bingo!" he calls out, pulling a 9mm semi-automatic, loaded with thirty rounds, out of the suspect's jacket.

"Everyone wants a gun collar. It's not enough to do a frisk of everyone. You specifically have to find a black man with a dark jacket, if that's the description over the radio," Patrick says. Placed in handcuffs, the teenager and the three cops drive back to the precinct, another gun off the streets. Seventeen years old, the young man says he was only bringing the gun to a friend—it isn't his.

Sergeant George Schulz greets them inside the precinct. He had once approached a Hispanic man with wavy hair who bore all the signs that are suspicious to police officers. Looking around nervously, the man kept his hand in his pocket, protecting its contents. Did he have a knife, a gun? Schulz stopped to question the man, who reluctantly removed his hand from his pocket. Out popped the head of a live chicken he had purchased from a neighborhood poultry market.

Word reaches the precinct that a young black man, who had shot and paralyzed an officer, has been killed in a motorcycle accident.

"The only thing better than that was if he were paralyzed," says Alan Patrick.

"A lot of people have the eye. I spoke to the occupant of a car. The occupant was being very furtive. He struggled, broke free, and ran down the block. When he came in for inventory, we found eleven kilos of cocaine. We went to a suppression hearing. The judge determined that, other than talking to the individual, there was no obligation to respond." At another car stop, Patrick says, "[The driver] went to get out of the car. I'm trained to control the situation. It's a tactical car stop. He pushed the door open. He reached under the seat. It was enough for me to search the car. If we come up with contraband, we're allowed to seize. The judge threw it out and ignored the fact that we had $250,000 worth of cocaine."

Quality of Strife

Sleepy men with brooms sweep storefront sidewalks on Third Avenue. Smoke shops selling marijuana open the gates of their stores with the regularity of honest businesses. Heroin addicts cluster in McDonald's in groups of three or four, clutching hot coffee in swollen hands and gossiping in raspy voices, before they saunter off to their methadone programs. Cops call them Methadonians.

Officers David Laredo and Robert Smith walk by storefronts that sell drugs, day after day. They cannot simply close them. They are not allowed. Investigations can take up to a year. Neighborhood residents don't believe it.

"They ain't done nothing about it," complains one woman. "They know what's goin' on so it must be okay."

One cop blames the bureaucracy: "The Corporate Council does their investigation. You [go] see the lawyer because you're aware that there's a problem. The City says that you have a case. The landlord is getting the rent. What does he care? The landlord will say, 'I don't know. There was no illegal activity.' The landlord said they shut the place down. They closed the front gates but only opened it for specific purposes. If you watched the area, you knew it was open at certain times. The owner said the place was closed. You go back and forth."

No patrol officer walks in and closes down storefront drug dealerships.

Fearing leaks and interference, commanding officers and cops often aren't informed that special police narcotics units, the ATF, and the FBI are in their precinct until the end of an investigation. In April of 1996, narcotics cops seized $12 million worth of cocaine in candy boxes at Kennedy Airport. The investigation began at 110th Street and Lexington Avenue when one of the suspects arrived with a rented truck to pick up his haul. Cocaine was picked up in Columbia and dropped off in Puerto Rico, where it was taken to a San Juan candy company. Cocaine was packed with sugar wafers, cookies, and chocolates and shipped twice a month on American Airlines flights to New York, where it was received and eventually unloaded in the Hunts Point section of the Bronx. The cocaine ended up in Queens and was distributed throughout New York City. The two suspects, one from Queens, and one from the Bronx, came to pick up the candy in their rented truck. For five months, from this operation alone, over $100 million of cocaine came through 110th and Lexington Avenue.

The FBI, together with organized crime and special narcotics units of the Police Department, deals with the bigger businessmen; the 23rd Precinct deals with the smaller merchants and their customers. The Street Narcotics Enforcement Unit (SNEU) of the precinct targets buyers and sellers of drugs, and drug paraphernalia, setting up surveillance from rooftops, windows, and vans. Drug dealers, clever and expert, always seem to be a step ahead, moving inside to apartments when the streets are picked clean.

Every single block in East Harlem is a potential drug location, with the exception of Mount Sinai Hospital. Two hundred thousand heroin addicts, a quarter of the country's total number, live in New York City, the heroin capital of the United States.

Some cops feel that the end justifies the means. A search deemed illegal means that the suspect is free but the guns and drugs are seized—half a victory. As is seizing and smashing a scale to weight the cocaine. Says a sergeant: "They don't have an arrest. A cop takes a moment to smash the scale. He had no authority to touch the scale, but he knew what he was doing. Now, they can't package any more stuff for a few hours."

Meanwhile, the City focuses on "broken windows" quality-of-life violations, which include littering, drinking beer and other alcoholic beverages in public. In East Harlem, where the community faces much larger problems, the cops and their enforcement of these violations is looked upon as a nuisance. "You mean to tell me on a hot summer day, you can't drink a beer in front of your own apartment?" says one man, incredulously. "That's shit, man."

People gather outside for a cold beer, sitting on stoops, or on park benches. On the upper East Side, in the 19th Precinct, neighbors gather in bars and pubs. In East Harlem, residents gather on corners to exchange news, play dominoes, and drink beer. "They're not bothering anyone," says one resident. "It's a cultural difference."

"It's really not bothering anyone," a cop agrees. "But we have to enforce the law."

In East Harlem, the commerce of heroin, cocaine, marijuana,

crack, and angel dust is big business, as entrenched as the housing projects. East Harlem has been enveloped by drugs for de-
cades. Drugs wiped out layers of Puerto Ricans in the
neighborhood during the 1960s. Junkies shot up heroin, sitting on
curbs. One Hundredth Street between First and Second Avenues
was once an open-air market for drugs. The majority of crimes in
the precinct are related to drugs: one drug dealer robs another,
junkies burglarize apartments, trying to get money for crack.

Even in East Harlem, summonses for traffic or quality-of-life
violations are at a premium; City Hall's mission to bring civility
and order back to New York City has forced the police to issue
summonses for unleashed dogs, open beer containers, bicycle riding on sidewalks—offenses which used to draw a warning or were
ignored. Score is kept by arrests, not convictions.

Quality-of-life crime comes to East Harlem in a major way in
Operation Taco, which starts, appropriately enough, at lunch time.

Sergeant Rich Romano's mission, along with a team of cops
from the 23rd, is to confiscate unlicensed taco stands and food
vending carts. These colorful mobile lunch counters—minus running water, restrooms, food hygiene and other amenities—dot
Third Avenue, dispensing tacos, grilled meat, hot dogs, and ices.

"We once went on a call to an apartment, I forget what for,"
says Officer Carlos Zerega. "It was the home of one of the vendors.
All the meat that they were going to sell was hanging from the
ceiling in strips; it was covered with flies."

Proprietors without permits collect monies from unsuspecting
diners who don't know or care about food preparation or that sales
and income taxes aren't being paid. But the role of the police—
as defined by the law and by a mayor interested in quality-of-life
in the City—is to check for permits and, if there are none, to
issue summonses and remove the offending food carts. The owners
all knew Sergeant Romano from his frequent patrols up and down
Third Avenue, and he warns them week after week that they need

the proper paperwork. The captain, he says, wants the stands removed.

Romano, a tall, dark-haired, angular man, who always seems lost in thought, approaches a taco stand with a trailer hitch on 104th Street, at the corner of Third Avenue. Accompanied by Officer Zerega, who translates, he asks a chubby woman wearing a dirty apron and stirring a pot for her business license. She says she has none. Before they can continue their conversation, a woman in an oversized navy blazer and glasses runs out of a nearby building.

"Why are you doing this?" she yells at Sergeant Romano. "This is their business! They're not bothering anyone!"

Romano tries to explain, but she won't listen. "They're not robbing anyone!" she insists, standing less than a foot away from him. "They're just trying to make a living!" He steps back and doesn't answer, and turning, instructs his men to take the cart. It's loaded onto a police truck, to be stored at the pound in Queens.

Illegal vendors sell everything from tacos to perfume to videocassettes, flowers, ices, balloons, underwear, jewelry, and wicker baskets in East Harlem, blocking sidewalks and taking business away from legitimate business owners who pay taxes and who struggle to keep their businesses open. Some of the vendors' wares, cops say, is stolen property. Most neighborhood residents look for their bargains without questioning, praising a man or woman for earning a day's pay.

"They think this is a shopping spree," Sergeant Romano says. "The guy next door pays taxes, registers his business. I understand that people are trying to make a living."

"Clean it up, guys," Romano warns a group of African men selling videocassettes. "This is a warning. Next time I'm gonna give you a summons and I'm gonna take your property."

"If the store owners don't want it, then I'll ask them to move. Some are illegal," says Officer Zerega. "You've got some people selling stuff for ten, twenty years. They say, 'Now you're going to tell me I can't do it, that I need a permit.' They don't understand that."

"I'm not too fond of it," admits Sergeant Romano. "In reality, they are breaking the law. When the peddler says he's trying to support his family and kids, that's when you feel bad. Every time we go collecting, the public is not too fond of us. When we take the taco stands, people want to know why can't you get the drug dealers. 'Leave him alone,' they say. If you stop to tell them that store owners are complaining, they don't want to hear it, so you're better off to ignore it. People don't want to give up their stuff, which is understandable, and they start giving us attitude, so we bring them in for disorderly conduct. They can get their stuff back," he says. "It's vouchered downtown to the property clerk. But the fines are hefty, a minimum of two hundred and fifty dollars. A lot of guys don't show up to court; it's cheaper for them not to show up. They know that the majority of the time the judge is on the cop's side, because they can't come up with a permit."

He turns to a peddler selling T-shirts from a table. "Two strikes, Charlie," Sergeant Romano warns him. "I warned you twice in the last week. Save yourself some aggravation. Don't come back here. Next time you'll get arrested."

"I hate doing this," he says, under his breath, then: "You can't be here. Captain's orders." He calls out to an African man selling brass statues from a black cloth spread out on the pavement. "The captain doesn't want you out here," he says to another man, selling plastic-wrapped sweaters for two dollars. "I've warned you a hundred times. You're not supposed to be here," he says, as a crowd gathers. He and Zerega pack the clothing in black plastic bags, Zerega writing a summons when they finish.

Community Policing, Sergeant Romano's unit, is considered a plush assignment. Unlike patrol, Community Policing officers or beat cops are not committed to the police dispatcher and their police radios, and are not accountable for their time. Walking the beat is considered a reward for time on patrol, but the inclusion of rookies to the unit through contacts or the whim of the captain creates resentment and concern among older, more experienced cops. One brand-new beat cop, standing on Fifth Avenue and 106th Street, hears the radio call of a cop chasing a man with a gun thirty blocks away. He turns off his radio "so he can't hear us," pulls out his 9mm pistol, his finger on the trigger, and creeps into the bushes of Central Park. "Just in case he runs this way, I'm prepared," he explains. How will he know if the gunman is coming this way if his radio's off?

"Don't worry, I'll know," he answers as he scrambles around the bushes like a kid playing cops and robbers.

Dave Argentina, a more experienced beat cop, with a quiet, firm demeanor, has made forty-six arrests over several months, effectively removing drug buyers from two buildings on his beat. He has enlisted landlords to join the Manhattan District Attorney's Trespass Affidavit program, under which anyone not having business in the building could be asked to leave. If they fail to produce identification, they can be arrested. As a result, drug trafficking has diminished in these buildings. Their hallways are clear; the front doors are locked. For his efforts, he is called "the captain's pet" and "not a team player" by his colleagues. "Some people don't make any arrests. Why be on the job if you're not going to do your job?" he asks, shrugging his shoulders.

Beat cops, when they are not patrolling their territory, are often organized into special assignments like Operation Taco. They travel in vans to pick up students who ought to be in school; they stop drivers for unbuckled seatbelts, missing headlights, and driving while intoxicated. They write summonses for double-parked cars, arrest people in drug sweeps, and fill patrol cars during vacations and when the precinct is short-handed. They check to be sure that bodegas are not selling beer to underage kids and drugs or drug paraphernalia—vials, scales, plastic envelopes—to both residents and outsiders.

These bodegas were once owned and operated by the original Puerto Ricans who settled in the neighborhood. Most moved on to bigger and better businesses and now they are mostly owned and operated by Arabs selling everything from triple-X-rated tapes to cans of tennis balls and potato chips behind plexiglass. St. Ides beer is cheap; two sixteen-ounce containers sell for ninety-nine cents. Bodegas carry individual packets of Kool Aid, coconut candies, audiocassettes, containers of Clorox in the window, Black Love incense, Melody Farms ice cream, and rolling paper, presumably for cigarettes. A jumbo microwaved cheeseburger sells for $2.22, Krasdale 12 super maxi pads for $1.99 are piled next to rat and mousetraps, large containers of pickles, and plastic rain hats. Bon Ton cheese cubes are priced at twenty-five cents and so are the slot machines that pay out fifty cents. One bodega sells moldy oranges, dirty food cooked on a toaster, dusty packages of Jell-O, Instant Quaker Oats made in Colombia, and Lady Irma knee-high socks. An altar is nailed to the wall. Cops say that stores are forced by organized crime to keep the slot machines and threatened if they don't.

In one, an old black-and-white television with bad reception plays a Spanish soap opera next to men drinking beer underneath a sign saying, WARNING: NO DRINKING IN THE STORE. You can purchase plastic Uzi water pistols, coffee pots, wigs, dice, soda, dirty meat, plastic handcuffs, and diapers.

Signs proclaim, NO BEER SOLD TO ANYONE UNDER 21. NEED I.D. One of the bodegas on 110th and Lexington sold beer to a twenty-year-old police cadet during one of the 23rd Precinct's undercover operations.

"You people keep fuckin' up. You can't sell beer to these people," complains Officer Robert Smith to the Arab sales clerk. "I hate to do this because they kept me warm during the winter," he says, "but you gotta do it." The six-foot-tall Smith stands in the entranceway, his arms folded across his chest, his legs spread apart, to prevent customers from entering as his sergeant speaks to the sales clerk.

A black man, carrying a paper bag, tries to push past him.

"It's closed," Officer Smith says, as if the man should know better.

"Excuse me," the man says, attempting to maneuver around him.

"It's closed," the cop repeats more firmly.

"Fuckin' po-lice," the man replies, before leaving.

Inside the store, Sergeant Steve Ringe questions the man behind the counter as he writes the summons. "When's your birthday?"

"I don't know," the man replies without expression.

"What month? Warm or cold?" the sergeant continues, standing next to packages of moldy pies.

"I don't know."

Next to the counter is a stand holding X-rated and hit movies on videotape with badly photocopied labels that violate copyright laws. Stacking them in black paper bags, the police will voucher them and use them as evidence.

"The man doesn't have I.D. and we're looking for a business license," Sergeant Ringe says. The man is handcuffed. "No license. It expired in March," Ringe says. "We can have the whole place shut down. You have to ask for I.D. when you sell beer," he informs the man. "You are required to ask for I.D."

In the bodega, Officer Smith opens a door to a cabinet, revealing scales, empty crack vials packaged with cardboard wrappers, multi-colored plastic tops, different colored plastic heroin bags, laxatives to cut the cocaine and heroin with, even an order book of supplies. The clerk and the contraband are transported back to the precinct house. Each item is accounted for and vouchered by the property clerk. More than half of the muster room is covered with thirty-two large plastic trash bags filled with these items. "And all this is a misdemeanor," Smith notes.

Sergeant Ringe, a well-informed spokesman, popular at community meetings, describes one of the illegal businesses in the neighborhood: numbers.

"These people think it's not a crime. One cop was telling me that, growing up, his mom used to take numbers over the phone. Someone was paying her a hundred dollars to answer the phone. They don't think of it as a crime," Ringe observes.

The numbers game is well organized. Networked. Spanish Raymond, a well-known local criminal, is out of jail and back in numbers. "He has the policy locations and big operations. We closed one of his stores. But he has an employee network, so they'll set up shop in another location. They constantly rotate around. 'You closed down my shop, now I'm going to open a beauty supply shop with a different owner,' " Ringe explains. "The landlord is supposed to take action against his premises. Once you make him aware [of drugs or other illegal activity], he has to take action. If he fails to take action to evict, we can instigate eviction proceedings for him, but then the costs will be levied against him. We can close the premises down and that will cost him in rent. We've taken action against owners of the store. This illegal activity is terminated on behalf of the City. The premises will be closed for one year. We have to identify the person committing the criminal act. We don't do searches. We take the contraband, but I can't break down walls."

Some legitimate businesses are of interest to the police as well.

"Santeria plays a major role in East Harlem," explains a detective who specializes in researching and investigating it. "The botanica plays a major role, just as the psychotherapist applies to the upper middle class. The psychology and spiritual elements are very important in terms of mental health. It's something that they can go to. Just knowing starts the healing process.

"A snake is always an evil thing, live or dead. Turtles can go both ways. Frogs are seen as an evil element. Seahorses are considered evil, especially if someone leaves one in front of your door and they want you dead. Technically, you're not supposed to take money for giving advice at the botanica. The Gods will get offended. You buy fruits or vegetables. Some people make thousands and thousands of dollars off of clients." At the upper end of Central Park, by the lake, he notes, "you see a lot of fruits and vegetables. You can see the animal carcasses. They just use normal cats and dogs, stray animals. You get your human sacrifice, too," he adds.

"I'll tell cops not to touch religious items in an apartment or you'll have a problem. People will turn on you. Some people will tell you not to touch any of this for health reasons. You never know if it's blood or a liquid. Every major psychiatric ward knows about Santeria. If that is an element, they have a list of people that they call. That's standard. If you don't believe, it's no big deal. Items do not work if they're not blessed. Every item is empowered. If they have blessed it, then it's supposed to work, like a Ouija board. Some drug dealers practice Santeria. Basically a good god, Eshu, protects the road, transporting drugs. Most of the Latin Kings practice Santeria. People blame Santeria for everything. They will bless an individual and they get paid very, very well. They want someone dead and they will bless a hit man. Some people don't care. They think that nothing will hurt them. They sprinkle holy water on weapons. Some pray to a god who deals with jail and legal cases. Some cops believe in Santeria."

Lowlife

Officer Walter James edges the car slowly up First Avenue as Sergeant Matt Kennedy scribbles in his memo book, looking up to eyeball a man panhandling from a wheelchair next to Metropolitan Hospital. He waves him off with his hand. "You look forward to your days off," says James. "I couldn't give two shits once I leave here."

"Me, either," Sergeant Kennedy adds, looking up at a group of teenagers down the block. "In the suburbs, you might have law-abiding citizens. In the city, everyone is out for themselves. The majority of people in the city probably like cops, but you never hear about it. You see the worst of things and no one appreciates it."

James and his sergeant often go out together after work. Whenever James suffers from a painful hangover, the sergeant drives him. "A lot of cops go out after work because they want to be accepted," James says. "They've heard stories about people not being down with everyone. A lot of people are single and still live at home," adds the twenty-nine-year-old James, who is single and lives with his parents in Queens.

Pop! Pop! Gunshots.

James' and Kennedy's heads swivel as they try to figure out where the gun and the shooter are. But in the maze of streets and rooftops running east, west, north, south, it is almost impossible to tell. Kennedy holds his police radio up, listens for the dispatcher's directions. The dispatcher, in a room at Police Headquarters, only has information if a neighborhood resident thinks it important enough to call 911. The radio is silent.

"The day comes that I have to fuckin' shoot someone—if I believe it was the correct thing to do—then I'll get another job." James groans.

He steps on the gas and they roll through the dark streets, occasionally spotting the lights of a patrol car at another intersection. One pulls up alongside theirs. Sergeant Kennedy has to sign—"scratch"—their memo books. He looks up as a cop in a Halloween clown mask hands over his book through the window.

"Indeedy," Sergeant Kennedy remarks, straight-faced, "anyone can be a New York City Police officer."

James waves a hearty hello and the two cars separate. "There's a lot of problems on this job," the five-year veteran says. "A cop will ride with an older guy who says, 'Hey, kid, join the circus!' One: the job is young. People should be at least twenty-five with at least two years of college. Two: people get married for all the

wrong, fuckin' reasons. Three: a lot of people take financial bur-
dens that are ridiculous. They buy a car, have kids, pay for that
through their salary, pay child support. It takes a toll. They feel
there's no end to it. Then you come to work, help someone save
their fuckin' marriage, and you're supposed to be a guidance coun-
selor, to protect the neighborhood.

"We have a fucked-up way of hiring. They make a big deal out
of the screening process. If you have a misdemeanor, you can be
hired. I don't agree with the way the job goes about hiring people.
I think it's fuckin' ridiculous."

James pulls up to three black teenagers standing in front of a
building on 115th Street, another drug-prone location. They hide
their blunts underneath the lid of a garbage can as the police car
approaches. James looks over. "Where do you live?" he asks.

"Over there," answers one, pointing to the Lexington Houses.

"Is that your dog?"

"Yeah."

"Take your dog, after it pisses and craps, and get off the corner."

Kennedy and James continue on their journey, stopping three
blocks south on 112th Street at a red light. A young black man
in his late teens, wearing black jeans and a black sweater, walks
over to their car with his hands up.

"Why are your hands up?" Kennedy asks, confused.

"I don't want to get shot."

"Move along," Kennedy says, looking past him at two men in
the shadows.

"I was in jail unjustly," the man offers.

"I can't help you," Kennedy says, waving him away. He turns
to his partner. "They didn't want to sell heroin because there's a
police car on the block."

As the man walks away, hands in his pockets, Sgt. Kennedy, a
cop for ten years, says, "I don't like when they come to the car

with their hands in their jackets. They look like they're carrying things."

Officer Walter James, the son and grandson of New York City fire lieutenants, has recently returned to riding in a patrol car. "I had to pick one—the Police or Fire Department," he says. "I needed a job that was consistent with solid benefits. What better place than the City of New York? For some reason I didn't feel like following my father and grandfather. They were both fire lieutenants. It was too much to follow. You're looked at like so-and-so's son. Fuck that. I don't want to have anything to do with that."

James's uniform, hair, outward demeanor, and physique are as polished and trim as those of any career military man. Unfortunately, over the past few months he has not fulfilled the Police Department's expectations of making two or three arrests a month. While the outcome of an arrest is not recorded—whether the suspect pleads guilty, innocent, plea bargains, or manages to have the case thrown out—the number of arrests belongs to each cop. Because of James's lack of activity, he says, he's been removed from patrol as punishment and given the least desirable footpost in the precinct—directing traffic at the congested intersection of 96th Street and the FDR Drive. After three weeks, his ban from patrol is lifted without explanation. But instead of riding with a partner, he is assigned to drive the sergeant. He speeds past the boundaries of the 23rd Precinct into the 19th to get gas; precinct pumps are out of order. James started as a rookie in the 19th Precinct.

"They felt like we were their own private police," he says of the wealthy Upper East Siders. "They demand it because they're paying your salary. One lady had her wallet picked out of her purse on the bus. She expected us to find the bus. She said, 'If you leave right now, you can catch the bus.' I said, 'Lady, we can't just do that.' No matter where you go some people have some sort of resentment," he sighs. "In East Harlem, they feel that you're there to harass. They think we're picking on them, that we decided out of the blue to bother them. A guy's dead. He's a shit drug dealer. People won't come out and say it openly for fear of retaliation. More people are carrying guns in this neighborhood. Guns are for a purpose here. They're used for protection.

"In the Nineteenth, people listen to you. There are a lot of professional people and working there is a great way to learn how to speak to people. I'd rather start there than here. I respond to people. If someone talks to me politely, I'm polite. If they're fuckin' rude to me, I'm fuckin' rude to them. A lot of people don't have jobs here. They wake up in the middle of the day. They've probably had a bad experience with the police because they've had a lot of contacts. In the Nineteenth, they have little contact, if any, with the police. In East Harlem, when you do show up, you're bothering people and they don't give two shits whether you show up or not. Any kind of contact is always negative. They can't do what they want. Their way is to take it out on the uniform. After a while, there's a big wall. For you to say, 'How's it doing?' they look at you like you're crazy," he says, opening his window and nodding at an older Hispanic man with a bag of groceries in one hand, leading a five-year-old with the other. "How's it going?" he asks politely. The man looks at him like he is crazy. "They see people being arrested. They see people resisting, and they call it 'police brutality.' The next cop that asks them a simple question, it becomes a bigger project."

As they turn the corner, they pass a dark-skinned man about twenty-five on the corner of 111th Street. "That's some of the drug dealers hanging on the corner," James points out. "He's fuckin' nervous, too. They're out here every day, just like we are. We see their faces every day. They see our faces every day. It's like the Cold War."

A black man in a wool cap waves them down.

"They're trying to kill him on One Hundred Sixteenth Street," he warns.

"I didn't see anyone out here," Kennedy says, looking around.

"But they're trying to kill him."

"Who?"

"These people on One Hundred Sixteenth Street."

"What people?"

"He's walking to the subway."

"It's going to be a long day," groans James.

Another patrol car pulls up.

"How ya doin', Sarge?" the driver asks.

"What's up, buddy? Who you out here with?" Kennedy asks.

"All the lowlifes. I just gave a summons to a guy pissing on a wall."

The radio is dead. The car pulls to the curb in the moonlight. James says, "Working the four-to-twelve or an odd tour has a bearing on people going out. It means [you'll have] a lot more single people, a lot of people in makeshift relationships, the early stages of divorce . . . it just causes problems. Alcohol seems to be a big part of it. There seems to be a lot of social events—PBA, clambakes, precinct functions, Christmas parties—you always have a lot of cops with an interest in drinking. The next thing you know there are twenty cops in a bar. But I think we have more of a fuckin' sense of humor than anything. Two or three DOAs and that depresses you. If it was to bother someone it's very hard to tell. Everyone knows if you say you're having a problem, you're going to have to give up your gun. Everyone knows your business. There's no fear in going on a gun run—no fear in doing that. It's a fear in helping themselves, of not being in control. Cops don't like to be out of control," he says quietly.

"Out in the street, I would never question another cop. Even if I thought something was wrong, I wouldn't back down. For the most part, people will go along. I did not get into this job to question other cops," he says firmly. "I'll be damned if I put my life in jeopardy. The vast majority of police officers are going to back up a police officer. You make a decision and hope to God it's the right one."

A woman in an old sweatshirt and with most of her teeth missing passes by, the acrid smell of beer an overpowering perfume. "An alcoholic thinks he's above a junkie. You come looking to buy drugs, here's someone he could look down at," James says. "I haven't seen a drug dealer move out of the ghetto yet."

Sergeant Kennedy and Officer James pick up sushi and egg rolls for their meal and eat in their patrol car facing the East River.

"There's a great deal of freedom in the Police Department. I like the days off," Sergeant Kennedy says, in between bites. "The whole operation isn't going to come to a standstill. If I die today, you'll find someone to replace me.

"I found that cops would be my best friends and my worst enemies. They are culled from different parts of society. I found the sincere ones and the worst phonies. I'm kind of indifferent dealing with the public. I find myself picking up where parents have failed. I don't take it personally, but I am the symbol of authority. I have to instill authority. I walked a footpost in Hunts Point. There was so much drugs. It was like being a marshal in the Wild West. I was *it* out there. I saw cops who did not want to do anything. No one threw bottles or things from roofs because I would beat them down. I made a name for myself. I did a lot of yelling. I was not afraid of getting CCRBs [civilian complaints]. I took the lead. None of my collars—perps—had to be hospitalized or receive medical treatment. I didn't take bullshit from anyone. I'm not out there to wrestle with people. I'm basically a nonviolent person. It's a lot worse if you walk away. You have to deal with it a second time. When I go out there, I want everyone to know who I am and what I'm doing."

"Shots fired, One-oh-six and Third," the dispatcher announces.

Dime

"**L**ike any profession, you're not going to give up someone else unless you have to. We're always in the public eye. It goes on in any profession if you're close with someone. You're not going to give someone up. The blue wall of silence is never gonna change. 'Rat' stays with you during your whole career, that you're a rat. No, I wouldn't say anything."

"I'd cover for a cop if he or she shot at someone, because Department guidelines leave a lot to be desired. Things can be erratic on this job. If I can say I didn't see anything or not say anything, I will. You don't have time to think things out, to react. I was going to shoot a sixteen-year-old girl who wanted to off her boyfriend. I told her to drop the knife. I waited and waited and waited. I was a hair away from shooting her. She had a butcher knife in her hand and she was going to stab him. The mother came out of nowhere.

Dead heroes are bullshit. If I had to take her out I would have. It doesn't mean I have to sacrifice myself. They'd give me a plaque and forget about me."

You lose part of yourself with this job," says Bob Kirby. "The killings, the dead bodies, people jumping from bridges, kids burned, stabbed, beaten, people just not caring. You can't be the same person you used to be when you started."